An OPUS book

A History of Western Philosophy: 5

THE EMPIRICISTS

R. S. Woolhouse is Professor of Philosophy at the University of York. His other books include *Locke's Philosophy of Science and Knowledge, Locke,* and *Descartes, Spinoza, Leibniz: The Concept of Substance in Seventeenth-Century Metaphysics.*

OPUS General Editors

Christopher Butler
Robert Evans
John Skorupski

OPUS books provide concise, original, and authoritative introductions to a wide range of subjects in the humanities and sciencies. They are written by experts for the general reader as well as for students.

A History of Western Philosophy

This series of OPUS books offers a comprehensive and up-to-date survey of the history of philosophical ideas from earliest times. Its aim is not only to set those ideas in their immediate cultural context, but also to focus on their value and relevance to twentieth-century thinking.

A History of Western Philosophy: 5

The
Empiricists

R. S. WOOLHOUSE

Oxford   New York

OXFORD UNIVERSITY PRESS

Oxford University Press, Great Clarendon Street, Oxford OX2 6DP

Oxford New York
Athens Auckland Bangkok Bogota Bombay
Buenos Aires Calcutta Cape Town Dar es Salaam
Delhi Florence Hong Kong Istanbul Karachi
Kuala Lumpur Madras Madrid Melbourne
Mexico City Nairobi Paris Singapore
Taipei Tokyo Toronto Warsaw

and associated companies in
Berlin Ibadan

Oxford is a trade mark of Oxford University Press

First published 1988 as an Oxford Univesity Press paperback
and simultaneously in a hardback edition

British Library Cataloguing in Publication Data

Data available

Library of Congress Cataloging in Publication Data

Woolhouse, R. S.
The empiricists.
(An OPUS book, History of Western philosophy; 5)
Bibliography: p. Includes index.
1. Empiricism—History. 2. Philosophy, Modern—17th
century. 3. Philosophy, Modern—18th century. I. Title.
II. Series: OPUS. History of Western philosophy; 5.
B816.W66 1988 146'.44 87–7818

ISBN 0–19–289188–X (pbk.)

7 9 10 8

Printed in Great Britain by
Biddles Ltd
Guildford and King's Lynn

To David Norman

Acknowledgements

I am immensely grateful to Richard Francks for his painstaking, generous, and invaluable help with early drafts of this book. My gratitude is also due to Susan Mendus for her constructive comments on the final draft.

Contents

1

Introduction

This book belongs to a series devoted to the history of philosophy from earliest to latest times, and the 'empiricists' referred to in its title do not include all those who have been so called. Like its companion *The Rationalists*, its period is bounded by an earlier volume on the Renaissance and later ones on philosophy since 1750.

According to Bertrand Russell, 'one of the great historic controversies in philosophy' is that between empiricists—'best represented by the British philosophers, Locke, Berkeley, and Hume'—and rationalists—'represented by the Continental philosophers of the seventeenth century, especially Descartes and Leibniz'. The controversy, as Russell describes it, concerns the relation of our knowledge, ideas, and thought in general, to experience on the one hand, and reason on the other; each school seeing more, or less, importance in the one or the other of these possible sources of knowledge and ideas.

The idea that the English Channel has intellectual significance was perhaps shared by Voltaire, who saw European and British philosophers as having temperamentally different styles. But the philosophers Russell mentions would not have accepted it. Berkeley and Hume were indeed both British, but they would not have seen themselves as falling, along with Locke, into a school diametrically opposed to Descartes and Leibniz on the Continent. Though Locke undoubtedly set many of the parameters of their thought, Berkeley and Hume are as often critical of him as they are in agreement with Nicolas Malebranche, a French Cartesian. Pierre Gassendi was French too, but Locke's philosophy shows marked similarities with his. Nor would these philosophers have characterized themselves or others primarily by these labels. They would have spoken first of Cartesians, Platonists, or Aristotelians, not of rationalists or empiricists.

The fact is that the systematic use of the labels 'empiricist' and 'rationalist' is a product of nineteenth-century histories of philosophy, which saw seventeenth- (and eighteenth-) century philosophy in idealized terms, as a conflict between two opposing schools which reached some sort of resolution in the philosophy of Kant.

In these idealized terms, an empiricist will seek to relate the contents of our minds, our knowledge and beliefs, and their acquisition, to sense-based experience and observation. He will hold that experience is the touchstone of truth and meaning, and that we cannot know, or even sensibly speak of, things which go beyond our experience. A rationalist, on the other hand, holds that pure reason can be a source of knowledge and ideas; what we can meaningfully think about can transcend, and is not limited by, what we have been given in experience. On the face of it there is something to be said for both of these views. It is only from experience that I know that unprotected iron rusts in the rain; whereas I know by the necessity of deductive reasoning that the external angle of a triangle is equal to the sum of its internal opposites. The empiricist's reply to this is that geometrical truths are trivial consequences of our own initial definitions; and in any case we would not, independently of all experience, have any ideas in terms of which to reason and think in the first place. The rationalist's is that isolated pieces of factual belief are insignificant compared with the certainties of a rational system of knowledge, such as geometry gives us; as for our initial ideas, some of them are innately built into the mind and do not come from experience. The limits of knowledge and of intelligibility are not set by experience.

Besides being a *theory* about the basis and origin of knowledge and the contents of our minds in general, empiricism is also sometimes a *methodology*. Someone could follow, or even explicitly favour, observational and experimental procedures in the search for knowledge, yet hold no theory about how exactly knowledge, and the ideas in terms of which we express it, are related to our sensory input. Of all the 'empiricists', Locke stands out for his lengthy and detailed presentation of just such a theory. Bacon, on the other hand, is almost purely a methodologist. He enthusiastically advocates and describes certain empirical procedures by which knowledge should be sought; but he does not reflect on the relationship between knowledge and ideas on the one hand, and experience on the other, in the way that Hobbes, Gassendi, and Locke increasingly do.

But, although there are elements of empiricism in their thinking, the philosophers discussed in this book are not idealized types, they are not exemplars of, or official spokesmen for, a laid-down creed. For one thing, they were living people with a wide range of intellectual interests and concerns, and it would often require reconstruction and distortion to make it appear that their focus was always on questions about knowledge and its relation to experience. For another, even when they are more or less directly concerned with such questions, or even when they merely imply answers to them, we should not expect that what they say will necessarily fit neatly and tidily into these pre-set categories. Hobbes might as easily have appeared with the 'rationalists', and this book's inclusion of certain philosophers as 'empiricists' is, to a considerable degree, a matter of convention. The book will be more concerned with explaining just what the views of various philosophers were, than with attempting to justify and explain their being so classified.

Whatever their other interests, questions about knowledge certainly were, in the seventeenth and eighteenth centuries, a major concern of 'rationalists' and 'empiricists' alike. This comes out in their frequent discussions of, and references to, the question of the so-called 'criterion of truth'. It comes out in their discussions of certain sceptical arguments which purport to show that knowledge is not something that is humanly attainable. And it comes out in their discussions about the proper method to acquire knowledge. Their concern with knowledge arose in the following way.

Up to the time of the Reformation in the sixteenth century, the 'rule of faith', the test of truth in religious matters, had been a matter of Church tradition, Papal decrees, and Church Councils. These were the source of religious knowledge, and provided the criteria for distinguishing truth from heresy. Martin Luther broke

with the Catholic Church in holding that neither the Pope nor
the Council was infallible. The test and source of religious knowledge, he said, was not the word of the Church and its leaders; it
was the Scriptures as understood by a faithful and sincere reader.
A disagreement of this sort is clearly quite radical. When people
disagree their difference can usually be settled by appeal to some
agreed test or criterion, a procedure or an authority. But when
the disagreement concerns the tests or criteria themselves, matters
are obviously less straightforward, and less easily settled.

Some thirty years later, in the 1560s, the flames of this religious
controversy were fanned and extended by the appearance in
France of the first printed editions of the work of Sextus Empiricus, an Hellenic writer of about AD 200. These are a main source
for our knowledge of the history of Greek scepticism, a history
in which Pyrrho of Elis is an important figure, and which ends
with Sextus himself. In his *Outlines of Pyrrhonism* Sextus defends
the conclusion of Pyrrhonian scepticism, that our faculties are
such that we ought to suspend judgement on all matters of reality
and content ourselves with appearances; we cannot even be
certain, as were Socrates and the Academic sceptics, that we know
nothing. He correspondingly attacks the view of the dogmatists
that we can know the truth about things as they really are. An
important feature of this attack is the question of 'the criterion
of truth', a general question of which Luther's question about
'the rule of faith' is, in effect, a particular case. The dogmatists
believe that truth can be discovered. How, then, is it found? What
is its criterion? What is the basis on which what is true may be
distinguished from what is not?

The two criteria usually offered were reason (the criterion of
the ancient rationalists) and the senses (the criterion of the ancient
empiricists). Sextus offers arguments to show that neither of these
criteria is satisfactory, and accordingly presented an intellectual
challenge which is a part of the explanation why so many came
to be interested in questions of method. As the sceptics claimed
to show that knowledge is not possible, it is incumbent on any
who think it is to formulate and describe the method by which
they think it is attainable.

Besides the sceptical problems about the 'criterion of truth' and the possibility of knowledge, another part of the background to the seventeenth-century concern with knowledge, and the method of acquiring it, was a dissatisfaction with what Aristotle had taught about these matters. Aristotle's influence on the seventeenth century, the period with which this book is mainly concerned, is difficult to overestimate. The reasons for this go back to the collapse of the Roman Empire, when the intellectual and scientific traditions of classical Greece came to be lost sight of in Western Christian Europe. It was not until the time of the Crusades, in the eleventh to thirteenth centuries, that many of the works of the classical authors, and of Aristotle in particular, began to filter back from the Arabs who had kept the classical tradition alive. The vast store of learning and intellectual speculation contained in them far surpassed the achievements of the West. The enormous impression they made produced a general conviction in the intellectual superiority of the ancients, and a belief that their writings contained all knowledge. By the seventeenth century, however, this Aristotelian tradition was increasingly under attack, even though there were still many 'peripatetics', and 'scholastics' or 'schoolmen', who carried it on. Aristotle could never be ignored, however, and even the thinking of those who rejected him was shaped by his teachings.

The very attitude of unthinking respect for an accepted authority, which had been adopted towards Aristotle, was one thing which came under attack. People's minds, it was felt, had been enslaved by the past, and what it taught had been taken on trust. Doctrine had been handed down and unquestioningly adopted, improperly assimilated, and left undigested by the juices of living and individual understanding. As Bacon complains, 'men have been kept back as by a kind of enchantment from progress in the sciences by reverence for antiquity, by the authority of men accounted great in philosophy'. As a result, 'Philosophy and the intellectual sciences ... stand like statues, worshipped and celebrated, but not moved or advanced'.

As for the content of traditional teaching, it was thought to lack substance and significance; it had brought philosophy to a standstill. Its categories, terms, and whole conceptual apparatus led to empty controversy instead of constructive argument. Thus, according to Bacon,

that wisdom which we have derived principally from the Greeks is but like the boyhood of knowledge, and has the characteristic property of boys: it can talk, but it cannot generate; for it is fruitful of controversies but barren of works.... If sciences of this kind had any life in them, that could never come to pass which has been the case now for many ages—that they stand almost at a stay, without receiving any augmentations worthy of the human race; insomuch that many times ... what was asserted once is asserted still ... and instead of being resolved by discussion is only fixed and fed.

Some years later John Webster asked about the still-prevailing scholasticism, 'what is it else but a confused chaos, of needless, frivolous, fruitless, trivial, vain, curious, impertinent, knotty, ungodly, irreligious, thorny, and hell-hateth disputes, altercations, doubts, questions and endless janglings?'

One particular piece of Aristotelian teaching which came in for these accusations of verbal triviality was the doctrine of *scientia*, which provided an account of science or knowledge, an account which will be discussed in more detail in Chapter 4. Our present-day conception of 'a science' as an organized body of knowledge is a descendant of this doctrine. Particularly in so far as knowledge of nature is concerned, much of the detail of the Aristotelian doctrine has been dropped. For this reason our 'natural science' is descended not only from *scientia*, but also from the newer conception of 'natural philosophy', which people like Bacon, Hobbes, Gassendi, and Locke, developed in reaction to the Aristotelians.

According to the Aristotelians, *scientia* is knowledge which, by virtue of the way it is structured, gives an understanding of why certain facts necessarily are so. This is done by explaining them in terms of their 'causes'. One would have 'scientific understanding' of iron's rusting in the rain when one had demonstrated the necessity of its doing so as a conclusion of a syllogistic argument, amongst whose premisses is a definition or account of the 'form', 'nature', or 'essence' of iron. Such a definition was meant to capture what iron really is, not merely how the word 'iron' is used, and was said to be arrived at by intellectual intuition after observation of a few instances. The syllogistic demonstration of which it forms a premiss involves 'causal' explanation, because 'forms', according to an Aristotelian division, are one of four sorts of 'cause'.

In fact, to speak of *causal* explanation here is somewhat redundant. An 'explanation' shows that something is so because of something else, and a 'cause' was taken to be whatever followed any 'be*cause*'. It is for this reason that the Aristotelians came to distinguish four sorts of cause, four sorts of explanation of how something comes to be as it is: material, formal, final, and efficient. The bronze of a statue and the silver of a bowl are their material causes. The human shape of the statue and the roundness of the bowl are their formal causes; in a sense it is their shape that *makes* them what they are. Their final causes are the purposes for which they were made. And their efficient causes are the people who made them—out of that material, with that form, and for that purpose. Just as the man-made bowl is a function of material and a certain form, so, analogously and according to the Aristotelian 'hylemorphic' theory, all natural things are a function of 'matter' (*hyle*) and 'form' (*morphe*). Just as the bowl is a bowl because of its form, so it is because some naturally occurring thing has the 'form' it does have, that it is the kind of thing it is. Moreover, it is by virtue of its 'form' (or 'nature' or 'essence') that a thing of a certain kind has the properties characteristic of that kind. So the aim of the scientific syllogism is to demonstrate, on the basis of a definition or specification of a given form or nature, both that things of that form have the properties they do, and why they have them.

In the seventeenth century many came to feel that, with the possible exception of geometry, no 'science' as understood by the Aristotelians ever had been, or could be, produced. In particular, the rather rigid formalized account of *scientia*, and the complex logic for constructing definitions which accompanied it, did not seem to fit, or be suited to, the study of natural phenomena. It really turned attention away from such study and towards verbal classifications and arguments about words. Any definitions of 'forms' which were ever provided, such as that 'man is a rational animal', were surely merely verbal formulae; they were insufficiently related to actual realities, which needed to be studied in far more experimental and observational detail. Finally, it was felt that it was hopeless to appeal to 'forms', as understood by the Aristotelians, if one wanted to explain and understand the properties of things. The explanatory structure of the material world was best seen in 'mechanical' terms, in terms not of the hylemorphic theory, but of another ancient theory, that of the Greek 'atomists', Leucippus, Democritus, and Epicurus. According to this, the properties of natural things result from the collisions and interactions of the minute atoms of which, the theory proposed, matter consisted.

Though the details of the theory of *scientia* came to be rejected, the general idea that knowledge, to be properly 'scientific', ought to be systematic and organized, and that the aim of the study of nature should be a knowledge of causes, was retained. But because of its Aristotelian overtones, there was a tendency, more marked in 'empiricists' than in 'rationalists', to avoid talking of 'science' in the context of knowledge of nature, and to speak instead of 'natural philosophy'. This means, of course, that 'philosophy' was not what it is now, a term for a specialized study of a certain range of ideas and questions. Just as 'natural philosophy' was knowledge of nature, so 'philosophy' was a generalized term for the product of any serious intellectual inquiry and investigation.

The philosophers of ancient Greece were not the only ones who set the parameters of seventeenth-century thought. Naturally, as the century progressed, those who came first in it had an influence too. In particular, much discussion went on in terms set by René Descartes, who is often spoken of as 'the father of modern philosophy'. Were it not that he conventionally belongs with the 'rationalists' of the era, it would have been proper that more be said of him in this book than actually is. Though neither immediately nor ultimately so influential as Descartes, Francis Bacon is another significant figure who stands at the beginning of early modern, or post-Renaissance, philosophy. To him we now turn.

2

Francis Bacon (1561–1626)

Francis Bacon was born in London in 1561 and died there in 1626. His father was Sir Nicholas, Lord Keeper of the Great Seal of Elizabeth I; his mother Anne Cooke, a well-educated and pious Calvinist, daughter of Sir Anthony Cooke. His contemporary biographer, William Rawley, remarked that, with such parents, Bacon had a flying start: he had 'whatsoever nature or breeding could put into him'. So, having through his life practised as a lawyer, and been active at Court and in Parliament, Bacon had risen by the end of it from Gentleman, through Knight, to Viscount, and from Barrister, through Attorney-General, to Lord Chancellor. Alongside of this, his devotion to more scholarly matters meant that his total written output runs to a dozen or so lengthy volumes.

Towards the end of his life, and not long after reaching the highest Crown legal position of Lord Chancellor, Bacon suffered public reversal. He was charged with accepting bribes from people whose cases he had to judge. He admitted the charges, though claiming that no bribe or reward had ever actually influenced him. A £40,000 fine and indefinite imprisonment in the Tower were remitted, but Bacon was officially excluded from public life. This enforced change of life obviously gave him more time for thinking and writing. Nevertheless, most of the work on which Bacon's fame as a philosopher rests was, incredible though it seems, done during his extremely busy public life.

Though Bacon appears to have felt that he was genuinely fitted for each of the two ways of life in which he excelled, the public one of law and politics, and the private one of study and extensive writing, his two sides do seem somewhat disparate. Perhaps they could be reconciled through the fact that in the latter he was essentially a propagandist for science and knowledge. In one way or another his writings all consist of plans for 'The Advancement of Learning'. As these plans often involved extensive collaboration and the creation of colleges, libraries, and laboratories, they depended on the kind of support and Royal patronage which Bacon, the public figure, was well-placed to obtain, and he often tried to do so. He was certainly conscious of this, and said he had had it in mind when planning his life. But if his rather severe Victorian critic Lord Macaulay is right, the mundane fact is that, despite his genuine scholarly concerns, he simply had a rather selfish and worldly interest in 'wealth, precedence, titles, patronage, the mace, the seals, the coronet, large houses, fair gardens, rich manors'.

Bacon was obviously an entertaining, civil, and witty personal companion, though he seems to have been somewhat cold-hearted and lacking in strong affection. He died, according to John Aubrey, the seventeenth-century biographer, as a martyr to the cause of scientific experiment—of cold and fever caught while stuffing a hen with snow: 'Snow lay on the ground and it came into my lord's thoughts, why flesh might not be preserved in snow, as in salt.' This well-known story loses some dramatic impact when one discovers that Bacon had already noted years earlier that 'cold preserves meat from putrefaction'.

Bacon either wrote in Latin or took steps to have his work translated into it. It was, as he says, 'the general language'. It was not until towards the end of the seventeenth century that English, which he thought too provincial, became an accepted medium for written thought. He said of a Latin version of one of his books, which he sent to the future Charles I, that it would be 'a citizen of the world, as English books are not'. The book in question was *De Augmentis* (1623), an enlarged version of *The Advancement of Learning* (1605), which was the first of his philosophical writings to be published, and the one largely responsible for his fame and importance. Along with it should be ranked the *New Atlantis*, written in 1610 but not published until 1627, just after his death, and his *Novum Organum* of 1620.

In 1592 Bacon wrote to his uncle, Lord Burghley, that 'I have taken all knowledge to be my province'. The attempt to solicit financial help, in which he was engaged at the time, was ill-judged;

his philosophical self-characterization was not. What he sought, beginning when he was only 24, was nothing less than a completely new beginning for knowledge: 'The Great Instauration', or Restoration, as he ringingly calls it in the preface to the *Novum Organum*. The ship sailing out beyond the Pillars of Hercules, which is pictured on the title-page, is a fitting symbol of his grand conception. According to classical myth, Hercules set the pillars up at the Straits of Gibraltar, the western entrance to the Mediterranean. Bearing the motto '*ne plus ultra*' ('go no further'), they marked the outer limits of the world. So far as the advancement of knowledge was concerned, Bacon wished to chart a route by which to go where no one had gone before.

His writings show a single-minded and persistent obsession with knowledge and learning in all of their possible aspects and modes. There are pages of painstaking and detailed records and expositions of things we know: facts about the wind ('wet weather with an east wind continues longer than with a west'); about the magnet ('there is no medium known by the interposition of which the operation of the magnet in drawing iron is entirely prevented'); about the phenomenon of life ('islanders generally live longer than those that live on continents'); or about density (gold, he tells us, is about thirteen times denser than raw calves' brains). There are lists and plans for things it would be good to get to know, covering almost everything, from the heavenly bodies, through the geology and geography of the earth, to basket-making. There are classifications of different sciences and branches of knowledge: knowledge divides into inspired divinity and philosophy; philosophy into natural divinity, knowledge of man, and natural philosophy; natural philosophy into metaphysic and physic; and so on, and so on. There are accounts of methods by which knowledge might be acquired and increased, recorded and stored, passed on and disseminated. There are ideas for libraries, colleges, and scientific societies. Finally, in the *New Atlantis*, there is a description of 'Solomon's House', an elaborate institution of workshops, laboratories, and libraries, all dedicated to the systematic and collaborative pursuit of knowledge.

Bacon's division of knowledge into Inspired Divinity and Philosophy is based on the idea that all knowledge is ultimately derived from one or other of two sources: it may be 'inspired by divine revelation', or it may arise from our senses of sight, touch, hearing, and the rest. The two sources and their products are quite distinct. Sensory experience, Bacon says, 'is like the sun, which reveals the face of the earth, but seals and shuts up the face of heaven'. His idea that study of the world will not tell us, beyond the bare fact of His existence, about God's nature and His plans, and that beliefs about them will not help us much in our investigations of the natural world, is one which can be traced back to William of Ockham. Bacon insists on it: 'Men must soberly and modestly distinguish between things divine and human, between the oracles of sense and of faith; unless they mean to have at once an heretical religion and a fabulous philosophy.'

Bacon says relatively little about Inspired Divinity; setting it aside, we are left with the thought that the source of the bulk of all the knowledge we have is our senses. But significant as this is, we should not place too much weight on it by taking it as a manifesto, a considered announcement of a developed empiricism of a theoretical sort. Unlike Locke, Bacon does not argue for some theoretical view that all of our knowledge ultimately derives from experience; unlike him, he does not go in for showing how sensory interaction with the world is necessary for, and results in, ideas and knowledge. His empiricism is methodological. It consists in his being a propagandist for empirical and observational knowledge, and in his provision of a systematic method for increasing it.

Apart from revelation, then, all philosophy, all human knowledge arises from the senses. It divides into three: knowledge of God, of man, and of nature. Though it can tell us nothing of His plans, observation of the structure and design of the world can show us the existence of God. By observation we may learn also about the physical and psychological aspects of man, both as an individual and as a member of society. Bacon's conception of 'Philosophy' is of course somewhat distant from and more general than ours, particularly when we think of the subject as taught in universities. But its third division, knowledge of nature or 'Natural Philosophy', is more familiar to us. The term is still in use for some university courses, and what Bacon means by it is very closely related to what we would now more easily call 'natural science'.

An evident Baconian characteristic is an enthusiasm for classifying, listing, cataloguing, and naming. Sometimes there is something almost primitive and magical about this; sometimes it merely gives a tedious and turgid portentousness to what he says. But if Bacon's classifications seem naïve and artificial this is in part simply because they are not ours. Despite being closely related, his natural philosophy, for example, is not identical with our natural science. He finds it important to distinguish knowledge of man from knowledge of nature. But now, after a further three hundred years of the history of thought, a history which notably includes Hobbes, Locke, and Hume, the distinction is often less marked.

Though an enthusiastic propagandist and spokesman for knowledge, Bacon nevertheless was not happy with the current state of natural philosophy. 'Let a man look carefully into all that variety of books with which the arts and sciences abound, he will find everywhere endless repetitions of the same thing, varying in the method of treatment, but not new in substance, insomuch that the whole stock, numerous as it appears at first view, proves on examination to be but scanty.' If one supposed that most of what there is to be known is already known, and has been since ancient times, this complaint would seem out of place. Once anything forgotten has been rediscovered in the works of earlier authors, there is room only for rearrangement and commentary. Indeed, up to Bacon's time this supposition had had some currency, partly as a consequence of the West's discovery of the impressive works of classical antiquity, which was mentioned in Chapter 1; partly, also, as a consequence of the fact that in Bacon's time many found it natural to think of the past as superior to the present. They believed, in general, that nature as a whole was in decay; in particular, that their intellectual abilities could never match those of the great minds of the past.

Bacon does not share this reverence for the past. He thinks that those who have it are guilty of both over- and underestimation. They overestimate the stock of knowledge that has been handed down to them, and they underestimate their own abilities and chances of adding to it. A few ancient authors should not be left to stand as boundaries, like the Pillars of Hercules. A proper respect for age ought not to lead to a regard for the so-called 'ancients'. In an often-repeated seventeenth-century image, Bacon says that he and his contemporaries are the true ancients. The world gets older each year, not younger; and those who come later stand on the shoulders of their predecessors, and see further. Indeed, the relatively recent inventions of gunpowder (fourteenth century), printing (fifteenth century), and the mariner's compass (thirteenth century), which made possible the great voyages of exploration and discovery—all inventions highly significant to the seventeenth-century mind—showed that advances were there to be made.

Another, and rather different, reaction which faced Bacon was that the poor state of knowledge was not worthy of remark or particular comment. As a result of exposure to the arguments of the Greek sceptics (mentioned in Chapter 1), many would have felt that the question, whether they or the so-called ancients were better placed to acquire knowledge, did not arise. All people alike are poorly placed. Of course the stock of knowledge is limited, for nature is complex and the human mind weak. It should be no surprise that knowledge is hard, if not impossible, to come by.

Bacon's reaction to the sceptics' arguments, which he said 'doomed men to perpetual darkness', is hardly one of sympathy. But he does not consider them in detail. It is not the un-attainability of truth that stands in the way of success in natural philosophy, but rather a failure to use the correct procedures of investigation. Certain 'Idols', or mistaken ideas and methods, have held men back. If they are removed, avoided, or given up, and the correct method understood and adopted, huge advances in knowledge could be made. Bacon's popular fame partly rests on his account of four classes of these 'Idols' which beset the mind, and in this case his often cumbersome terminology and classifications seem to have caught on.

Idols of the Tribe are mistaken ways of thought which arise from human nature as such. We are naturally prone to suppose more regularity in the world than there is, 'hence the fiction that all celestial bodies move in perfect circles'; we tend to see what supports our own conclusions and to ignore anything to the contrary. Idols of the Cave are intellectual faults and prejudices which individuals have as a result of their particular temperament or upbringing. Some are obsessed by this idea or subject, some by others. Some worship the past, others crave for change and novelty. The Idols of the Market-place are the pernicious influences which words and language can have over us. Our own categories impress us by their familiarity as being natural and correct; we continue to use words which are ill-defined, or are part of a false or outmoded way of thought.

These first three kinds of Idol obstruct discovery and learning. The fourth, Idols of the Theatre, are mistaken methods which have been followed in the pursuit of knowledge. Together with the correct procedure which Bacon will advocate, each of these mistaken ones all have in common some relation or other to experience. Their mistakenness or otherwise depends on just how they relate to, or deal with, experience.

This means, of course, that Bacon is not a simple-minded empiricist; knowledge, for him, is not straightforwardly a matter of experience as it happens to come. Empiricist he is in his anti-rationalist insistence that natural philosophy should not 'rely solely or chiefly on the powers of the mind'; empiricist he is in his insistence that 'to experience we must come'. We must not be 'pure reasoners'; they are like spiders making cobwebs 'out of their own substance'. But nor must we, ant-like, amass a 'mere medly and ill-digested mass' of experience and observations. We should be like bees, who not only gather material 'from the flowers of the garden and of the field', but also digest and assimilate it, transform it by their own powers. The method Bacon advocates is one which begins with experience, indeed, but with an experience which is guided by reason and understanding, and which is then properly appraised and digested by them. 'The information of the sense itself I sift and examine in many ways.' He insists on a 'league' between the 'experimental' (experience and observation) on the one hand, and the 'rational' (understanding and reason) on the other. It is from this combination that 'much may be hoped'.

Bacon's basic thought is, then, that the pursuit of knowledge has been largely unsuccessful because of mistaken approaches to experience and observation of the world. The 'sophistical or rational' approach has failed because of its over-hastiness to generalize on the basis of a few obvious experiences and observations. It spends too little time, or none at all, on the facts of experience, and moves on too quickly to abstract speculation. Those who have adopted it 'snatch from experience a variety of common instances, neither duly ascertained nor diligently examined and weighed, and leave all the rest to meditation and agitation of wit'. Bacon has the Aristotelians in mind here; he is objecting to that aspect of their account of *scientia* according to which real definitions of the forms or natures of things are arrived at by intellectual intuition, after observation of a few instances. Indeed, their theories as a whole had never much appealed to him. According to his biographer Rawley, it was as early as his Cambridge student days that he 'first fell into the dislike of the philosophy of Aristotle ... being a philosophy ... only strong for disputation and contention; but barren of the production of works for the benefit of the life of man'. The basic trouble was, Bacon says, that Aristotle 'made his natural philosophy a mere bond-servant to his logic'; 'demonstration by syllogism ... let[s] ... nature slip out of its hands.'

As a representative of the equally mistaken 'empirical school', Bacon cites William Gilbert, author of *De Magnete* (1600), an influential treatise on magnetism. His failure was not to neglect particular facts, but to exaggerate the importance of some of them. Whereas an Aristotelian might quickly leave behind the actual phenomenon of magnetism in his abstract generalizations about it, Gilbert and his followers saw everything as an instance of magnetism. It was the soul of nature, an ever-present active principle.

Bacon objects, finally, to those who mix superstition and theology with their endeavours in natural philosophy. In searching for the causes of natural phenomena they think in terms of divine purposes, rather than more immediately in terms of other natural phenomena. Alluding to number mysticism and the theory of forms, Bacon mentions Pythagoras and Plato; but he probably also has in mind the Aristotelians with their final causes, and other of his contemporaries such as Robert Fludd, the hermetic magician, who took natural science to have its basis in revelation.

Once these Idols are broken and removed, once mistaken methods and approaches are abandoned, the way will be clear for a satisfactory natural philosophy. Unlike the superstitious, we should direct our concern only to the natural world. But it will not be enough merely to take it haphazardly and as it comes. There was a vogue at the time for bestiaries and encyclopaedias which simply retailed disjointed information, usually of a fabulous kind, and Bacon rejects any such aimless gatherings. Not only must facts be collected with some further end in view, but also, avoiding the example of the sophistical and empirical schools, they must be used in the right way.

In general, then, progress in natural philosophy has been impeded because nature has been approached unsystematically and incorrectly. Bacon's aim is to describe a new and correct method. He conceived of its need, if not the actual method itself, quite early on, and he often speaks of the mind requiring a method as an instrument or help in its pursuit of natural philosophy. The current sorry state of affairs means that there is 'but one course left . . .—to try the whole thing anew upon a better plan, and to commence a total reconstruction of sciences, arts, and all human knowledge, raised upon the proper foundations'. 'It is necessary', he proclaims, 'that a more perfect use and application of the human mind and intellect be introduced.' Exactly what is the relationship between the method and the human intellect? Looked at in one way, it is simply a description of the way in which the mind would naturally work if left to itself, clear of all hindrances. But the doctrine of the Idols means that the human intellect suffers from corruptions, is not unhindered, and cannot go in for its 'true and natural work'. In another way, therefore, the method is a prescription, a set of mechanical rules which will enable the spell of the Idols to be broken.

Bacon's interest in the sources of error, and in a method for acquiring knowledge, is shared not only by other 'empiricists' in his century, but also by the 'rationalists' Descartes and Spinoza. They too had doctrines or accounts of error in their *Rules for the Direction of the Mind* (written 1628) and *Treatise on the Correction of the Understanding* (written 1660). Somewhere in the background against which this interest was worked out was, inevitably, the Aristotelian account of *scientia* or 'scientific understanding'. Aristotle's doctrine can be found in the *Organon*, his collection of logical works. This Greek word means an 'instrument' or set of methodological rules, and it is in explicit allusion to Aristotle that Bacon's method is presented in the *New Organon*, the second part of his projected *Great Instauration*.

This grand conception of a Great Restoration of Knowledge was never fully realized. Of its projected six parts, the first was to give no less than 'a summary or general description of the knowledge which the human race at present possesses'; the second, an account of Bacon's proposed method by which the stock of knowledge can be increased; the third, a record of 'the Phenomena of the Universe', as material to which the method was to be applied; the fourth, examples of this application; the fifth, examples of discoveries already made, to serve 'for wayside inns, in which the mind may rest and refresh itself on its journey to [the] more certain conclusions' which Bacon's method will produce; while the sixth was to be the climax of the whole—'The New Philosophy' itself. It was to set out all the fresh discoveries, the new knowledge 'which by the legitimate, chaste, and severe course of inquiry which I have explained and provided is at length developed and established'.

Bacon never really intended to complete this sixth part: it is, he said, 'both above my strength and beyond my hopes'; it was intended for future generations to achieve. The fourth and fifth parts seem not to have been written. A good idea of what would have gone into the first is given by *The Advancement of Learning*, and some progress was made with material for the third. Only the second part, dealing with Bacon's method, his 'True directions concerning the Interpretation of Nature', the *New Organon* itself, was ever really completed. Some of it is quite obscure to the modern mind; the beginning of the 'Second Book of Aphorisms' can be fully understood only against the background of alchemical theory. But Bacon's contemporaries did not always find it easy going either: King James I, to whom it is dedicated, remarked that 'it is like the peace of God, that passeth all understanding'.

The method is designed to give us knowledge of causes, for this, Bacon says, is the aim of investigation and interpretation of nature. While the method is new, the idea that natural philosophy is the investigation of causes is not. It has roots in the Aristotelian idea (mentioned in Chapter 1) that *scientia* is knowledge of causes. Bacon rejects the idea of producing syllogistic arguments from first principles or axioms, but retains, along with some Aristotelian terminology, its aim of achieving knowledge of causes. He also retains Aristotle's important distinction (outlined in Chapter 1) between four sorts of cause or explanation: material, formal, final, and efficient. Though, in common with many in the seventeenth century, he is somewhat sceptical of the search for final causes in nature, he divides natural philosophy into 'Physic' and 'Metaphysic', according as the concern is with material and efficient causes, or with formal and final causes.

His distinction between these two branches of natural philosophy is as follows. The whiteness of frothy water is produced by the intermixture of air and water. In knowing this, and thereby knowing how to produce such whiteness, we have physical knowledge of its efficient and material causes. But such whiteness is not only the product of the intermixture of air and water, for powdered glass is white too. What in the end 'constitutes' such whiteness, its formal cause, is the intermixture of two transparent bodies with 'their optical portions arranged in a simple and regular order'. Similarly, our knowledge that tea is produced by the infusion of leaves of a certain sort in boiling water is physical knowledge of material and efficient causes. Knowledge of the chemical composition of tea would be metaphysical knowledge of a formal cause.

In its more important aspect natural philosophy is 'metaphysical' for Bacon. It is knowledge, not merely of causes of any sort, but specifically of 'formal causes'. His method is essentially one for discovering 'forms'. Unfortunately, his explanation of this all-important notion of 'form' is sometimes obscure to us. It has lent itself to some disagreement and controversy. It might be said, for instance, that the above example of tea (which is mine and not his) erroneously over-reconstructs or goes beyond what Bacon actually says. In its allusion to a chemical theory which Bacon could not have had in mind, it certainly does. But whatever the difficulties of understanding his details, there is little doubt that the role played by the appeal to chemical structure in my example is entirely analogous to that which Bacon gives to his 'forms'. This is plain from both his example of the form of whiteness in frothy water and powdered glass, and the example of heat which he uses to illustrate and explain his method.

The aim, then, is the discovery of 'forms', either of simple qualities or phenomena such as whiteness, or a complex of properties such as tea. Such qualities or phenomena are called 'natures', and Bacon's lengthily developed example is, in fact, of a 'simple nature', heat. There are two distinct stages to the method. The first, the 'natural history' stage, consists of compiling three tables, or lists, on the basis of assiduous, painstaking, and extensive observation. The governing idea behind these is that the formal cause of heat, its 'form', will be present where heat is present, absent where it is absent, and will change in some way as heat increases or decreases.

Accordingly we must first compile a table of 'Essence and Presence', a list of all known cases of heat. The diverse miscellany of a mere couple of dozen cases Bacon himself gives is not meant to be complete; examples from it are the heat of the sun's rays, the heat produced by water on quicklime, and the heat produced by the violent rubbing together of stone, wood, or cloth. Next we need a table of 'Deviation, or of Absence in Proximity'. This, by contrast with the first table, lists cases where heat is absent. As such it could be endless; so it should include only those cases of absence which are 'most akin' to those of presence in the first list. Here Bacon cites the rays of the moon, which, by analogy with the sun's rays, we might expect to be hot. In fact the expectation is correct and Bacon's belief that there is no reflected solar heat in the moon's rays is mistaken. Finally, we need to draw up a table of 'Degrees or Comparison', cases in which the simple nature, heat, is found in varying degrees. For example, animals grow increasingly warm with increasing exercise, and warm in varying degrees from exercise and from pain.

The second distinct stage of the method, that of 'Induction', proceeds on the basis of these three tables. Bacon never fully described it, for his uncompleted *Novum Organum* ends with the never-fulfilled intention of discussing various 'Supports and Rectifications of Induction'. But his account is full enough to give a fair idea of it.

Given the copious data assembled in the three 'Natural History' tables, the aim now, of course, is to find a form 'as is always present or absent with the given nature, and always increases and decreases with it'. This, Bacon notes, is easily said. It is easy to say that one must survey the tables for something which can be identified as the relevant explanatory form. Doing it is more difficult. Acknowledging that our ideas and thoughts are often unclear, superficial, and limited, he recognizes that 'the way to come at it is winding, and intricate'. This may well be so. There may be no one single formal cause of the multifarious instances of 'heat' we have before us, for they may, in fact, be a collection of radically different phenomena. It may also be that there is a limitless number of possible candidates for a form which need to be ruled out, and so we never could come to a single end of exclusion and rejection. The promise that 'there will remain at the bottom, all light opinions vanishing into smoke, a Form affirmative, solid and true and well defined' is one that we may not always find easy to bring to fulfilment.

By means of the second table, it is relatively easy to rule some possibilities out: light and brightness, for example, cannot be the form of heat, for (or so he thinks) the bright rays of the moon are not hot. But to get further we shall need, as Bacon recognizes, to allow some 'indulgence to the understanding' and, as methodically as possible, use some conjectural imagination. So he draws attention to over twenty kinds of special 'Prerogative Instance' which should be looked for in the three basic tables, and which may provide hints as to the form in question. Thus, our understandings might be stimulated if, in the table of 'Presences', we look out for 'solitary instances' which exhibit the nature under investigation, but have little in common with other instances of heat. These will quickly and effectively rule out many of the possible candidates. We should also look out for 'shining instances' which 'exhibit the nature in question naked and standing by itself, and also in the exaltation or highest degree of power'.

Bacon does not demonstrate the use of such hints in his search for the form of heat, for it is before he gets to describing them that, as a first surmise, or 'First Vintage' as he nicely calls it, he hypothesizes that motion is the form of heat. That this might be so is 'displayed most conspicuously' in the perpetual motion of flames and of boiling water, but is indicated to Bacon by many other things. Consideration of these suggests to him not simply that heat is motion in general but is, specifically, 'a motion, expansive, restrained, and acting in its strife upon the smaller particles of bodies'. When Bacon says that motion of this kind is the formal cause of heat he is not, he explains, simply saying that it produces heat, as might an efficient cause. He is saying, rather, that this is what heat *is*—in just the way that we might say tea *is* stuff chemically composed or structured in a certain way. Lacking in detail as his 'first vintage' suggestion inevitably is, it is quite natural to connect it with more recent theories about the increase of heat in a material body being the increase in its molecular motion and kinetic energy.

Having seen what kind of result Bacon hopes to make available by his new method, we can now stand back to take some general stock. To begin with, it may be remembered that Bacon, dissatisfied with the contemporary state of knowledge, saw the need to 'commence a total reconstruction ... raised upon the proper foundations'. This serves to underline the fact that his method has two parts, each of which is of vital importance. First there is 'The Presentation of Instances to the Understanding'. This is the foundational or 'natural history' stage, in which we carefully and meticulously list facts concerning the particular nature under investigation; facts which, it should be noted, are to be collected, not simply from non-interventive observation, but also from active experiment. This production of 'natural histories' is the aspect of Bacon's two-part method which caught the imagination later in the century; and it is largely responsible for Bacon's classification as an 'empiricist'. But it would be wrong to think of Bacon, as is often done, as merely a collector of facts. He is certainly not one of the 'men of experiment' who list facts unsystematically, and for no particular reason (other than their entertainment value perhaps). Besides not being haphazard, Bacon's lists of his 'Tables of Presentation' form just the first stage of the 'Investigation of Nature'. The second, and constructive, stage without which the first would, for Bacon, have no point, is that of 'Induction', in which the instances of a nature are systematically surveyed in the attempt to discern their formal cause.

Bacon describes his method as 'mechanical'. It is meant to ensure that 'the entire work of the understanding be commenced afresh, and the mind itself from the very outset not left to take its own course, but guided at every step and the business be done as if by machinery'. But so far as the first stage of his *Novum Organum* or 'New Instrument' goes, this can hardly be so. Systematic and methodical we may try to be in compiling 'natural histories', but there can be no clear-cut procedure which will guarantee the discovery of fresh instances or tell us when the tables are complete. The second stage, that of 'Induction' proper, is not mechanical either. Even on Bacon's own admission it inevitably involves the use of imagination and conjectural hypothesis.

Bacon's answer to the scepticism which lay in the background against which he wrote, was to produce a method by which one could reach final and assured knowledge about formal causes. But even apart from the difficulties we have noted in the application of his method, and whatever the plausibility of his 'first vintage' idea about the form of heat, later revolutions and developments in science cast doubt on his hope of finality. The more limited claims we shall find in Hobbes and Gassendi square better with the way science has actually progressed and developed. According to them, any well-founded ideas we form about the workings of nature are essentially of a hypothetical character.

The actual development of science also brings to our attention Bacon's failure to recognize the importance of mathematics, which he treats not as a part of, but as an appendix to, natural philosophy. It is, indeed, a feature of later theoretical empiricism that pure mathematics is seen as merely the result of formal symbolic manipulation, and not as a substantive body of genuine knowledge. But Bacon's method for acquiring genuine knowledge is non-quantitative, and does not recognize that mathematical

manipulations can play an essential applied role in the 'interpretation of nature'. He appears quite ignorant of the fruits
already produced by Galileo's mathematical approach to nature,
and his purely qualitative account of how science is to progress
cannot make much sense of discoveries such as were made later
in his century by Newton.

Bacon's method was intended to be applicable not only to the
investigation of nature but also the study of man. Since some
aspects of the study of man, biology for instance, go easily with
the study of nature, the idea that it will help us to study human
beings is no more implausible than the method as such. But Bacon
seems to think that it will work also for what we would now call
the social sciences. This idea would be rejected by many later
thinkers (though not by Hobbes and Hume), who see radical
discontinuities between these two areas of study.

As we saw earlier, Bacon distinguishes between knowledge of
God's plans, 'inspired by divine revelation', and observation-
based knowledge 'arising from the senses'. But even though these
have no mutual relevance, and should not be mixed, the natural
world is still God's creation, and it has been thought impious or
somehow improper to study it; after all, it was a desire for knowledge that led to Adam's fall. As Bacon points out, however, 'it
was the ambitious and proud desire of moral knowledge to judge
of good and evil, to the end that man may revolt from God and
give laws to himself, which was the form and manner of the
temptation'. Adam's example gives us no reason not to pursue
natural philosophy. Nevertheless, the idea that the study of nature
is impious is one that many in the seventeenth century had to
face. One response to it was to suggest that such study is a form
of worship. Bacon's is to stress the need to study nature for the
right reasons.

Knowledge should not, he says, be pursued 'either for pleasure
of the mind, or for contention or for superiority to others, or for
profit, or fame, or power, or any of these inferior things; but for
the benefit and use of life'. These references to various improper
motivations are not merely casual, but have historical substance.
According to a basically Aristotelian view, science was something
which lay quite apart from the practicalities of life. It was essen-

tially the province and concern of those who had leisure for the development of the intellect by purely theoretical interests. Then, according to a Pythagorean tradition, one which permeated alchemy, knowledge was something arcane, which should be confined to a brotherhood of initiates, and kept secret from the masses. There were also charlatan alchemists who had used their knowledge for the sake of power, or fame, or notoriety, to produce startling, baffling, or amusing effects, such as may be seen now as parts of a conjuring show of 'magic', or in Royal Institute Christmas lectures. There was a tradition of interest in the unusual monsters and weird curiosities that can be found in nature. Bacon will have none of this. He insists that the mind is not lowered by a concern with everyday facts revealed to us by our senses. He insists, too, that they should be collected systematically, and for the purpose of further research. He insists that this should not be done by individuals or small select groups, but should be a truly collaborative affair, institutionalized and organized in a properly open manner. Above all, he insists that science does not begin when material needs have been satisfied, but should be pursued and used for the satisfaction of the needs of all.

Though this ideal of a practical goal for science is characteristically and paradigmatically Bacon's, it is not uniquely his. It focuses a tendency of thought already present in the sixteenth century and came to be embraced by others. Though it does not permeate all he says, Hobbes too insists that 'the inward glory and triumph of mind' which one may gain from the acquisition of some hard-won knowledge is 'not worth so much pains as the study of Philosophy requires'. The 'end or scope of philosophy' is, he says, its 'use to our benefit ... for the commodity of human life'.

Bacon divides natural philosophy into the 'speculative', or pure and theoretical, and the 'operative', or applied and technological. Quite clearly he is concerned for both: the knowledge of formal causes, to which his method is designed to lead, is pure and 'speculative'; while his stress on the practical usefulness of science, and his frequent discussions of the mechanical arts, shows a deep interest in the 'operative' and technological. But the two concerns are intimately connected. 'Speculative' knowledge of formal causes is desirable only because it will, of itself, lead to an 'operative' practical philosophy. Indeed, for Bacon there is some theoretical reason why this is so, for he often speaks of the discovery of causes as being identical with the discovery of a method by which we can produce desirable effects.

His account of the purpose of natural philosophy, and the details of the method by which it is to be sought, all naturally lead to the need for collaborative and suitably institutionalized scientific endeavour. The production of the 'New Philosophy' itself, all the discoveries which could be made by 'Induction' on a set of natural histories which capture all 'the phenomena of the universe', is, as he recognized, clearly beyond limited individual capacities. Besides which, knowledge and its practical benefits are for all to share, equally and alike. Towards the end of his life Bacon described, in his *New Atlantis*, a fabulous island in which knowledge is collaboratively sought after for its practical fruits. With its House of Solomon, a college devoted to 'the interpreting of nature and the producing of great and marvellous works for the benefit of men', it beautifully captures the vision of the practical application of science which energizes and enlivens all Bacon wrote. 'The End of our Foundation is the knowledge of causes, and secret motions of things; and the enlarging of the bounds of Human Empire, to the effecting of all things possible.'

Much of Bacon's time, during his enforced retirement after his public disgrace, was spent walking in the gardens of his estate at St Albans, conversing with friends who recorded his ideas. There was, so Aubrey tells us, one such companion Bacon 'better liked ... taking his thoughts, than any of the others, because he understood what he wrote'. This young man was Thomas Hobbes, the subject of the next chapter.

3

Thomas Hobbes (1588-1679)

Thomas Hobbes was born near Malmesbury in 1588, the son of the local vicar and his wife. The education he received culminated at Oxford and, like others both before and after, he was later to complain of the diet of scholasticism he was fed there. His time was often spent, he said, looking at maps in the local bookshops, following voyages of exploration such as those of Francis Drake.

After Oxford he was recommended as tutor to the son of William Cavendish, First Earl of Devonshire. This was Hobbes's eventual making. It resulted in employment and patronage for life. It introduced him to enlightened learning and a sophisticated life of foreign travel, and enabled him to move in the scientific circles centred round Sir Charles Cavendish. It also led to his enjoying a considerable reputation on the Continent, where he became acquainted with leading intellectuals such as Marin Mersenne, Pierre Gassendi, and René Descartes. His association with the Devonshires put him a little in public life, but for the main his world was, unlike Bacon's, largely an intellectual one. This is not to say it was quiet, for Hobbes published controversial *Objections* to Descartes's *Meditations* (1641), and was involved in acrimonious arguments with leading mathematicians about his attempts to square the circle. He also engaged in open controversy with John Bramhall, Bishop of Derry, about liberty and necessity. Against the complex political events of the Civil War (1642-51), Commonwealth, and Restoration (1660), his political and religious views, or their supposed implications, became notorious and were often vilified. His life of study and writing lasted until his death in 1679, at the age of 91.

Hobbes wrote sometimes in Latin, sometimes in English. By his middle years he had published little, and the ideas for which he is remembered did not begin to develop until then. He is most

famous for his political philosophy, which is embodied in his
Elements of Law, completed by 1640 though not published until
1650; in his *De Cive* ('On the Citizen') of 1642; and, in particular,
in his *Leviathan* (1651), a classic and perenially studied account
of man's move from a primitive state of nature, in which life is
'solitary, poor, nasty, brutish, and short', into an organized
society, with absolute power vested in the hands of a supreme
authority.

But *Leviathan* contains more than this, for political philosophy
is just one part of an ambitious and systematic three-part account
of the *Elements of Philosophy*. This deals with physics (with
'bodies natural'), with moral philosophy (with the 'dispositions
and manners of men'), and, finally, with political philosophy (with
the 'civil duties of subjects'). The later parts of this grand scheme
are logically dependent on the earlier so that, via his moral philosophy, Hobbes's political philosophy is ultimately dependent on
his physics. But a concern with the political unrest preceding the
Civil War caused the third part, *De Cive*, to be prematurely
'ripened and plucked' before the first two, *De Corpore* ('On Body',
1655) and *De Homine* ('On Man', 1657). The way in which the
three parts of Hobbes's system are meant to hang together and
the methodology by which they are worked out in detail is, of
course, most fully explained in its first part, *De Corpore*.

Hobbes complains of the lack of philosophical progress his
predecessors have made. Like farming, at a time when vines and
corn grew haphazardly here and there but were not cultivated,
philosophy has never been properly and methodically developed.
He recognized that some attempts had been made to cultivate the
seeds of Natural Reason into something worthwhile. But, with
some few exceptions, the main results had been disputatious wrangling. The natural philosophy of the ancient Greeks 'was rather a
dream than science'. Indeed, Hobbes says, 'I believe that scarce
anything can be more absurdly said in natural philosophy, than
Aristotle's Metaphysics.'

People are sensible to ignore these fruitless attempts at philosophy and 'content themselves with daily experience' and common sense, even if this is merely 'feeding upon acorns'. In the
hope of rectifying this unsatisfactory state of affairs, Hobbes

aimed to lay bare 'elements' or seeds from which 'pure and true' philosophy might grow, if carefully cultivated by a method which he will describe. 'Most men wander out of the way, and fall into error for want of method, as it were for want of sowing and planting, that is, of improving the reason.' Given a method, we can avoid mistaken ideas which, confirmed by the authority of the past, have taken deep root, like weeds in men's minds.

Hobbes's references to previous lack of philosophical progress and the disputatious wrangling of the prevailing scholastic philosophy, and his distaste for ideas based solely on the foundation of authority, are all reminiscent of Bacon. So, too, is his stress on the importance of finding, and following, a methodical route to knowledge. But Bacon and Hobbes were not alone in these ideas. It was shortly after his time at Oxford, on his first journey to the Continent, that Hobbes found that others were dissatisfied with scholasticism; and we have already noted that an interest in method was characteristic of the seventeenth century. So these ideas in Hobbes are an expression of a prevailing wave of thought, a wave which moves on through Gassendi and Locke.

Despite the aridities of scholastic philosophy, Hobbes did think that, over the centuries, the seeds of natural reason had borne some fruit. Three notable instances were the geometry of Euclid, the work done on the motion of falling bodies by Galileo, and the discovery of the circulation of the blood by William Harvey. Hobbes's discovery of geometry and his growing sense of the importance of motion in understanding the world were milestones in his intellectual development. Were it not for these he would not have produced any of the philosophy for which he is now remembered. Geometry and motion, both separately and intertwined, are a pervasive presence in his *Elements of Philosophy*.

In 1629 Hobbes returned to the Continent on a second tour, as tutor to the son of Sir Gervase Clinton. There, in Geneva, in a gentleman's library, he came across a copy of the *Elements of Geometry*, in which Euclid methodically organizes and systematically lays out a large amount of geometrical knowledge. The book was open at Pythagoras' discovery about the relative lengths of the sides of a right-angled triangle, and Hobbes was amazed by Euclid's proof of this complex idea. He was stunned by the rigour, clarity, and persuasiveness of the reasoning by which Euclid got this interesting theorem from a small initial collection of obvious axioms, elementary postulates, and clear definitions. From that moment Hobbes was, Aubrey tells us, 'in love with geometry'.

The idea that knowledge could be firmly established and disputes resolved if we began from clear beginnings always remained with Hobbes. The rational procedures of Euclid's *Elements of Geometry* inspired his own *Elements of Philosophy*. But, though it was Euclid's method that first inspired him, the subject-matter of geometry also caught his interest and was something he worked on throughout his life. One result he claimed was a proof that the circle could be squared. Given his initial thought that properly established geometrical results would not be disputable, it is ironical that this claim led to lengthy and acrimonious argument, and brought Hobbes into some disrepute. Finally, besides working on geometry and being influenced by its methods, Hobbes gives it, as the science of simple motions, a foundational role in the explanatory system of his *Elements*.

Not only Euclid, but Galileo too, had grown something worthwhile from the seeds of natural reason. In his attempts to understand the paths taken by projectiles and falling bodies, he had 'opened to us the gate of natural philosophy universal, which is the knowledge of the nature of *motion*'. Hobbes met Galileo, then an old man, in Florence in 1636, on a third visit to the Continent. But his fascination with motion, the 'gate of natural philosophy', had probably been with him from the beginning of that decade. It seems to have begun somewhat unexpectedly, when he was involved in a discussion which led to the question 'What is sense?' It occurred to Hobbes that since knowledge, whether systematically developed or not, begins with sense-perception, we should not pride ourselves on knowing much if we do not understand what sense-perception actually is. In thinking about this he 'luckily' (as he says) hit upon the idea that matter in motion is the key. His idea was not, simply, that matter in motion causes sense-perception, but that our sensory ideas just *are* motions in matter. This led him to think that everything, in one way or another, could be matter in motion. From then on, the idea of motion was always to the forefront of his mind and central to his philosophy.

Hobbes's two obsessions, geometry and motion, first came together in the early 1630s in a *Short Tract on First Principles*. This deals with motion and sense-perception, and is laid out, after the manner of Euclid, as a series of formal demonstrations. But they became even more closely connected when Hobbes began to think of geometrical figures in terms of the motions which would generate or produce them. Geometry itself was seen as the science of 'simple motions'.

Against the background of an Ockhamite distinction between faith, or 'inspired divinity', and philosophical knowledge, Bacon had divided 'Philosophy' into Natural Divinity, Knowledge of Man, and Natural Philosophy or Knowledge of Nature. Though not as obsessive as Bacon, Hobbes shares not only an interest in the classifications of areas of study, but also something of the actual divisions. He distinguishes 'faith' from knowledge proper which, as 'Philosophy', is divided into 'Natural Philosophy (or 'physics') and 'Civil Philosophy' (that which is concerned with man). In its turn, 'Civil Philosophy' is divided into 'Ethics' and 'Political Philosophy'. Hobbes's systematic conception of politics as dependent on ethics and then, via ethics, on physics, means that his natural philosophy must be looked at first and in most detail. But it is important to remember that not only 'natural' but also 'civil' philosophy comes under Hobbes's general definition of philosophy. Both of them are 'such knowledge of effects or appearances, as we acquire by true ratiocination from the knowledge we have first of their causes or generations: And again, of such causes or generations as may be from knowing first their effects.' Taken broadly, this view of philosophical knowledge as having to do with 'causes' shows Hobbes to be under the same Aristotelian influences as Bacon. There are, indeed, some similarities between them, but there are also differences.

By 'effects' or 'appearances', Hobbes means the ordinary observable qualities and properties of things or phenomena, or those things and phenomena themselves. So his 'effects' or 'appearances' are tantamount to Bacon's 'natures'. But when he speaks

of 'causes' he means, he says, either 'efficient causes' (which produce, or bring effects and appearances about) or, in the case of
what he calls 'entire causes' (the *combination* of causes *and* their
effects), a combination of efficient and material causes. Officially
he does not share Bacon's acceptance of formal causes, and even
his agreement with him about the relevance to human actions of
the final causes of Aristotelian tradition is qualified by the thought
that, in the end, they are reducible to efficient causes. The stress
on efficient or productive causes means that, though Bacon's
natural philosophy includes Divinity, Hobbes's excludes the theo-
logical study of a God that is eternal and ingenerate. Causation
for Hobbes is, of course, essentially a matter of motion, and his
example concerning the circle gives a good initial insight into this.
It also illustrates the associated idea, that philosophy is either a
knowledge of effects acquired from knowledge of generative
causes, or a knowledge of causes acquired from knowledge of
generated effects; and it also brings geometry into relation with
motion, for it describes geometrical figures in terms of the generative motions which cause them.

A circle is a shape on which all points are equidistant from
some point lying inside. This means we can work out how a given
circle might have been produced or drawn: perhaps it was traced
by the movement of one end of a rigid rod whose other end was
fixed, perhaps by a weight whirled round on string. When we
reason in this way, from the properties of the figure to possible
methods of its construction, we are reasoning from effects or
appearances, to their efficient causes or generating motions. But
suppose we have a figure which, though it looks perfectly round,
may in fact be slightly flattened on two sides, and in reality be an
ellipse. If we knew how it was produced, for example not by
moving a pencil round on one end of a taut thread, but along one
fixed at both ends, we could conclude that it really is an ellipse
and not a circle. Reasoning in this way, we acquire knowledge of
an effect or appearance from knowledge of its generative cause.

It is interesting to note that this example shows that what
underlies Hobbes's rejection of formal causes is, perhaps, no more
than an impatience with what the *Aristotelians* said about them,
and a desire to disassociate himself from that tradition. For it is

not clear that the generative or productive motions which 'cause' a circle really are put forward as 'efficient' causes; Hobbes has a tendency to speak of them in ways which make it not inappropriate to think of them in terms of some notion of 'formal' cause. His example makes it seem that the circle is not simply a detachable result of, or something which can be considered in isolation from, certain motions, but rather something whose very nature and properties are essentially tied up with its method of production. He seems to invite us to think of the circle as something which *embodies*, or is a continuing *expression* of, the motions which generate it; and this involves our thinking of those motions in a way which makes them less like efficient causes than like formal causes, at least as Aristotle intended them.

Philosophy, for Hobbes, is not simply knowledge of effects (or causes) based on knowledge of causes (or effects). To be 'philosophical', knowledge must be a product of reason or 'true ratiocination'. As such it differs from 'knowledge by sense'. Sensory images, which we refer to events outside us, are produced in us by motions. Some become associated in our minds when they recur in the same order. Because of the order of occurrence of certain images, we remember that fair mornings follow red evenings. Remembered sequences form our 'experience', the written record of which is 'history', both 'natural' and 'political'. Our own 'experience' and the authority of written 'history' give us prudence and foresight. They lead us to form expectations on the basis of present signs: a prudent man will take a violently red morning sky as a sign of impending storm. Hobbes would be foolish to deny the pragmatic importance of the knowledge given by wide experience and history, and he certainly does not do so. But he is at pains to stress that it is not philosophical knowledge, not true science. 'Sense and Memory of things, which are common to man and all living creatures' are knowledge, but 'because they are given us immediately by nature, and not gotten by ratiocination, they are not philosophy.'

Though true science, or ratiocinative knowledge, differs from experiential knowledge, it nevertheless begins with it. 'History', says Hobbes, is 'most useful (nay necessary) to philosophy.' Even so, the significance it has for Hobbes is nothing like that which it had for Bacon. The laborious compilation of exhaustive 'histories', or tables of instances, is an essential first stage of Bacon's method, the second of which consists in the scrutiny and examination of these many and varied instances to find their common form. So the examination of historical instances is never really left behind. They are either systematically collected, or studied for patterns and regularities. For Hobbes, however, though such 'histories' or lengthy records of experience are of great prudential value and interest, the application of his ratiocinative method does not demand them. The immediate sense-experiences with which his method begins are not part of a systematic record, and are very quickly left behind as one digs below their surface.

The distinction between rationalism and empiricism relates to a distinction between knowledge acquired by reason and knowledge acquired by the senses. Bacon is an 'empiricist', not because of some theory which shows that sensory experiential knowledge is superior, or prior, to knowledge acquired by reason, but because of methodological concern for advancing and improving the first kind of knowledge. Hobbes, on the other hand, is more of a theorist, less of a methodologist than Bacon: his distinction between experiential and ratiocinative knowledge is considered and explicitly made. He has, indeed, been further contrasted with Bacon by being called a 'rationalist', for he allows only the product of ratiocination or reason to count as 'philosophy' or 'science'. But he hardly dismisses experiential knowledge out of hand. It is, indeed, where philosophy must begin. To see what role this typically empiricist claim has in Hobbes's thought, we should look at the details of his account of philosophical knowledge, knowledge acquired by reason or 'true ratiocination'.

Hobbes's talk of 'true ratiocination' is an indication that he has some theory of what reason or ratiocination is, some explanation or analysis of it. According to this, ratiocination consists in 'composition' (or 'synthesis') and 'resolution' (or 'analysis'). These ideas have a long history going back to sources such as Aristotle, Archimedes, Galen, and Boethius. A classic and developed account of the resolutio-compositive method of reasoning was given by Zarabella, a member of the influential group of sixteenth-century thinkers associated with the University of Padua. With various mathematical refinements, it was this method that Galileo, one-time professor at Padua, used in studying the motion of falling bodies. It was also advocated by William Harvey, another ex-Paduan. Given his admiration for the scientific achievements of Galileo and Harvey, it is no surprise that Hobbes shares their methodological ideas.

The central idea of the resolutio-compositive method is that, to understand some complex matter, one must understand its parts, and how they fit together. So the initial stage in the discovery of the unknown cause of a given observable effect is resolution or analysis of the effect into parts. Then, once the causes of these parts are known, the cause of the original effect can be demonstrated by composition, or synthesis, of these partial causes. The distinction between discovery of causes by resolution and demonstration of the effects of certain causes by composition, was coupled with another, that between what is 'more known to us' and what is 'more known to nature'. Effects, or appearances, are immediately known to us by our senses. We are directly presented with them in our ordinary experience, and so must start with them in any investigation into hidden and unknown causes. But, though they are therefore 'more known to us' and come first 'in the order of our knowledge', effects or appearances in fact depend on, and are secondary to, their causes. Their causes come first 'in the order of things' and are 'more known to nature'. The method of resolution, which begins with effects and seeks for causes, was traditionally called the 'method of discovery, invention, or investigation'; so the direction or 'order of discovery' is from 'effects to causes'. The method of composition which begins with causes and demonstrates their consequent effects was called the 'method of proof or demonstration'; so the direction or 'the order of proof or of things' goes 'from causes to effects'. It was usually supposed that teaching should follow the order of discovery, for then the student is made to begin with familiar things.

These ideas can be found in Hobbes. The two directions of thought he distinguishes, from effects to causes, and from causes to effects, are discussed by him in terms of resolution or analysis, and composition or synthesis. There are differences of detail, of course; for example, he seems undecided about whether teaching should follow the order of discovery, or of proof. What is most important, however, is that he embodies them in a distinction, crucially important for his thought, between two sorts of science: 'indefinite science', which 'consists in the knowledge of the causes of all things', and the study of some 'limited' question about the 'cause of some determined appearance' such as heat. The first of these concerns the attempt to construct a general theoretical framework in terms of which we can answer the 'limited' particular questions of the second. 'Indefinite' science is obviously extremely important, for without some understanding of what general shape a causal explanation should take and of what concepts it should use, it would not be possible to give a detailed, or 'limited', causal account of the particular causes of some particular effect.

A 'limited' inquiry, one 'into the cause of some determined appearance', requires an initial process of resolution. For, though the particular thing or phenomenon in whose cause we are interested is presented in experience as a unified whole, it may in fact have 'parts' into which it can be rationally analysed. A man, for instance, is a whole whose parts are his having a certain shape, his being alive, and his being rational. Resolution into these parts is necessary in order to find their respective causes. Once the parts and their causes are known, rational synthesis, or composition, can take place. Given knowledge of the parts and their causes, synthesis will culminate in knowledge of the causes of the whole with which we first began in experience.

Clearly, though, doing this in any 'limited' particular case requires some background idea of what sort of thing a cause is, and how causes can be composed or combined. It requires, that is, that we have some 'indefinite' science. Hobbes outlines how the methical procedures of resolution and composition will result in such a science. He also, however, goes some considerable way towards actually producing the fundamental explanatory framework of this science which is a requisite for any 'limited' inquiry.

Like 'limited' particular science, general 'indefinite' science begins with the presentations of sense-experience, and with the analysis of composite wholes into parts. Its interest is not in the particular parts of particular kinds of thing, however, but in those parts which all material things have in common. Before we can know the cause of, say, rationality, by which men are distinguished from other things, we need to know the causes of those parts which all material things have in common, for example occupation of space, solidity, shape, and movement.

As in Euclid's development of geometry, these 'universal things' and other important basic notions need explication by clear definitions. Hobbes defines 'place' as the 'space which is possessed or filled adequately by some body', and 'motion' as 'the privation of one place, and the acquisition of another'. He says that some definitions, such as that of 'place', do not express the causes of what they define, for there are none. But other 'universal things', such as shape and extension, do have causes, and their definitions must express them. Basically, however, there is just one cause: 'the causes of universal things (of those, at least, that have any cause) are manifest of themselves, or (as they commonly say) known to nature; so that they need no method at all; for they have all but one universal cause, which is motion.' We are already familiar with Hobbes's fascination with motion, and how it seemed obvious to him that motion was the one basic cause. But if it is not by any application of the resolutio-compositive method that we know that all causation is a matter of motion, how can we be sure that it is? The value of this idea can really be judged only by reference to the value of the whole explanatory framework of 'indefinite' science, at whose basis it lies. Perhaps someone could come up with some better idea. But Hobbes is certain that as to 'those that say anything may be ... produced by ... *substantial forms* ... and other empty words of schoolmen, their saying so is to no purpose'.

In what way, then, is motion the cause of shape? We have already seen something of what Hobbes has in mind when we considered his idea of the generation of a circle. A solid cube has two-dimensional plane surfaces, and these have linear sides. One might define the lines which form the cube's sides as the shortest distances between pairs of points; but this would not express their motive cause which Hobbes conceives them to have. He defines a line as the result of 'the motion of a point'; a surface, similarly, is the result of 'the motion of a line'. Given these definitions we can ask, more specifically, just what motion of a point produces a straight line, and what a circular; what motion of a straight line produces a square, and what motion of a circle produces a sphere. From this 'kind of contemplation', says Hobbes, has 'sprung that part of philosophy which is called *geometry*'; and he gives some detailed results of his own geometrical contemplations (including an attempt to square the circle) in the second and third parts of *De Corpore*.

Geometry, then, is concerned with the production of figures by various motions. After it, says Hobbes, our thoughts should turn to what is, in effect, mechanics: 'the consideration of what effects one body moved worketh upon another.' We should consider what happens when one moving body comes into contact with another: 'what way, and with what swiftness, the invaded body shall move; and, again, what motion this second body will generate in a third.'

After the sciences of geometry and of motion comes 'physics'. Hobbes first describes this, in the introductory part of *De Corpore*, as a part of 'indefinite' science, the working out of a theoretical structure in terms of which particular 'limited' questions are answered. But later, when details come to be worked out, it appears as a part of the 'limited' investigation into the causes of particular effects. Its first concern is the phenomenon which, years earlier, had so intrigued Hobbes, and which engendered his interest in motion: the phenomenon of sense. In sense-perception we have a conscious awareness of material things around us, such as trees and stones, things which we can later represent to ourselves in memory and imagination. But not everything has this ability: the stones and trees which we can see and remember do not, themselves, have the capacity to 'represent'. Hobbes found it remarkable that some, but not all, things had conscious awareness and perception: 'Of all the phenomena or appearances which are near us, the most admirable is apparition itself ... namely, that some natural bodies have in themselves the patterns almost of all things, and others of none at all.'

From the point of view of Descartes, Hobbes's great French contemporary, this is not so remarkable. According to him, there is a strict dualism between mind, whose essence it is to think and perceive, and material, unthinking, extended body. So things such as ourselves, which perceive and have conscious awareness, do so because they are (or have) minds. They are of a completely different sort from purely material things, such as trees and stones, which are only objects of perception, and not themselves perceivers. In his *Objections*, appended to the first edition of Descartes's *Meditations* (1641), Hobbes rejects this. He does not deny the existence of mind, and he does not deny that it is the province of mind to think and perceive. But he does say that mind is nothing essentially different from body, and is, in fact, 'nothing but the motions in certain parts of an organic body'. According to this materialistic point of view, sense-perception is a matter of motion in the body of the perceiver. Objects outside of a perceiver generate motion, which is propagated through sense-organs to the heart and the brain. Because the parts of our bodies already have their own natural motion, there is a reaction to the motion produced from outside; and from 'the reaction ... a phantasm or idea hath its being'. It is because this reaction is directed outwards against the invading motion that the phantasms are experienced as though they were the external objects which initially caused them.

As noted, Hobbes seems undecided whether 'physics' (which includes his explanation of sense-perception) is included, along with geometry and mechanics, as part of the basic explanatory framework which he calls 'indefinite' science. He is perfectly clear, however, that 'indefinite' science is as I have just described it: a basic explanatory framework. He is perfectly clear that it is in the terms provided by this framework that we are able to answer any 'limited' question about the causes of particular phenomena. 'If a cause were to be rendered of natural appearances in special, as what are the motions and influences of the heavenly bodies and of their parts, the reason hereof must either be drawn from the parts of the sciences above mentioned, or no reason at all will be given, but all left to uncertain conjecture.'

In a manner more or less true to this claim, Hobbes devotes the last part of *De Corpore* to answering some particular questions about the motion of the planets, the tides, the weather, and gravity. Rather than follow him into this detail, it is more important here to underline an important general characteristic which Hobbes says the claim has.

Bacon's method was aimed at discovering the formal causes of particular phenomena. He believed that, by its means, we could arrive at certainty on such matters. But, besides the fact that the details of his method cannot be read into many of the advances made in the sciences, his promise of certainty has come to seem inappropriate. Theoretical explanations in the sciences tend to be of an essentially hypothetical nature. Other than the fact that they provide a satisfactory explanation, there is often no independent test of their truth. The suggested causes of a given phenomenon cannot always be independently observed, and so it is hard to rule out the possibility of there being explanations alternative to the one proposed. This is recognized by Hobbes's method. Unless we explain in terms of a framework based on the idea of the motions of material body, we are left with 'uncertain conjecture'. But even explanations in such terms, however certain they may be, are still 'conjecture'. 'There is no effect in nature which the Author of nature cannot bring to pass by more ways than one.' Use of the explanatory framework provided by his 'indefinite' science, together with the application of the resolutio-compositive method to particular observed phenomena, can only result in a hypothesis about its unobserved generative causes. Hobbes is quite explicit about this. All we can find out 'by the appearances or effects of nature, which we know by sense, [are] some ways and means by which they may be, I do not say they are, generated'. Beginning with the phenomena of sense, and by the use of our explanatory framework, we form hypotheses about their causes. These hypotheses can be tested against further experience and experiment, but hypotheses they remain.

Having reached some understanding of Hobbes's method in terms of its application in natural philosophy, we should recall that that subject, which deals with 'bodies natural', is simply one part of philosophy as such, and not the only part to which the resolutio-compositive method is to be applied. Its importance is that the other parts depend on its results for their complete explanations. They are, in their order of dependence: moral philosophy or ethics (which deals with 'the dispositions and manners of men'), and political or civil philosophy (which deals with 'the civil duties of subjects'). *De Corpore* contains only hints about these sciences, and their further development is in the other two parts of Hobbes's *Elements of Philosophy—De Homine* and *De Cive*.

Natural philosophy, or that part of it which is physics, will already have dealt with man to some extent, in considering the phenomenon of sense-perception. Moral philosophy, then, deals not with man's ability to 'represent' in perception, but with what Hobbes calls the 'motions of the mind'—desire, aversion, love, and benevolence. In studying these to find their causes we need to have done some natural philosophy, because these motions of the mind have their causes in sense and imagination. Just as Hobbes rejects Descartes's view of sense-perception as having to do with an immaterial mind, so his moral philosophy is purely materialistic, and appeals only to the idea of matter in motion.

Hobbes had learnt from his scientific hero, Harvey, that one of the motions in the body is that of the blood circulated by the heart. Like Harvey, he took the heart to be 'the original of life', and of crucial importance. It is 'the fountain of sense', for, by the 'vital motion' it produces, it governs what we perceive, think, feel, and desire. Motions from outside of the body often affect this 'vital motion', either helping or hindering it, and our awareness of these changes constitutes pleasure and pain. Learning from experience which things help or hinder the blood's motion, we come to develop appetites and aversions; we come to hope for what produces pleasure, and to fear what produces pain. In Hobbes's view, humans always act according to desires, and so always act so as to produce the increase in vital motion, which is pleasure.

On the surface of it, Hobbes's view of human nature as being completely egocentric is open to objection. Is there not such a thing as pity? Are we not sometimes benevolent towards our fellows? Anyone who finds Hobbes's view intellectually attractive will easily hit upon his thesis that someone who feels pity is simply moved by the self-centred thought 'that the like calamity may befall himself', and that people are benevolent only because this produces self-satisfaction. But the arguments of Bishop Joseph Butler, in his anti-Hobbesian *Sermons on Human Nature* (1726), suggest that the structure of human nature is more complex than this. One might do things out of a self-loving pride, but this is not benevolence; and though a benevolent person may gratify himself, this is not what he is aiming at, and is not the principle of his action.

It does seem possible to act on desires in a free, and relatively deliberate, way. In an extreme case, someone may act on them for the reason that, or on the principle that, 'a little bit of what you fancy does you good'. It does not seem that we necessarily are always simply taken, let alone overtaken, by our desires, so that they act themselves out in us as the force of the wind acts on a leaf. But the having of a principle of action, as opposed to the unreflecting impulsive acting out of a desire, has, in fact, no place in Hobbes's scheme (unless such principles are taken simply to be settled general desires). This is made clear in his controversy with John Bramhall, Bishop of Derry, on the subject of free will. According to Hobbes, we act 'by a certain impulsion of nature, no less than that whereby a stone moves downward'. For him, there is no faculty of the will. There is no such thing as deciding to do something, at least as this is usually understood. What we might think of as a process of deliberation and choice about our desires is, for him, simply the interplay and jostling of desires amongst themselves; and what we call 'will' is simply the desire that wins. But though desire determines actions in this way, there nevertheless is, argues Hobbes, a sense in which we can be free. Indeed, unless our desires do determine our actions, we are not free. There is no loss of liberty in being carried along on our strongest desire, even when, because of the external circumstances of physical threat, that desire is to turn away from satisfying some other desire. We are unfree, not when our strongest desire is displaced by an even stronger one, but when it is thwarted by external circumstances and becomes impossible of realization.

It is plain from all of this how moral philosophy is taken to depend on natural philosophy. The phenomena it studies, such as pity and benevolence, are explained in terms of a basic desire for pleasure, and aversion to pain, and in their turn these are explained in terms of the 'vital motion' of the blood. In short, 'the dispositions and manners of man' have their causes in motions, the complexities of which are the province of natural philosophy. In a similar way the phenomena of political philosophy, 'the civil duties of a subject', are, we shall see, reduced to, or explained in terms of, their causes in our basic desire for the pleasurable enhancement of the blood's vital motion.

It might appear that, in order properly to understand the moral causes of political phenomena, we need in the end to have understood the natural phenomena which cause moral phenomena. In fact, however, this is not Hobbes's view. He does not think that we need to have studied, in moral philosophy, the reduction of the 'motions of the mind' to natural philosophy in order to understand, in political philosophy, the causes of 'the civil duties of a subject'. For the 'motions of the mind', our desires and aversions, and what they may lead us to do, are not theoretical constructs known only by 'ratiocination', and introduced as an intermediary stage in the reduction of political to natural philosophy. They are known 'by the experience of every man that takes the pains to observe those motions within himself '. It does not take the explanations of moral philosophy about the relation of our desires and aversions, and hopes and fears, to the motion of the blood, to tell us that 'unless they be restrained by some power, [men] . . . will always be making war upon another'. This 'may be known to be so by any man's experience, that will but examine his own mind'. Political philosophy can be 'grounded on its own principles sufficiently known by experience'. So, although the events leading up to the Civil War made it seem desirable to Hobbes to write *De Cive* before the completion of *De Homine*, his finding this possible was not inconsistent with his conception of a three-part ordered system of *Elements of Philosophy*.

Hobbes was especially proud of the political part of his contributions to philosophy. Galileo had already opened the door to natural philosophy, and Hobbes supposed he was following Gilbert, Kepler, Gassendi, Harvey, and Mersenne, through it. But it was he himself who, he says, opened the door to political philosophy. He claims to have been the first to produce any. Indeed, he thought *De Cive* contained things of a rather different nature from anything so far in political philosophy: it contained *demonstrations* of its conclusions.

Apart from its demonstratively worked-out 'indefinite' framework, natural philosophy is essentially hypothetical. The phenomena it explains are given to us in experience; they are not produced by us, their causes are not directly knowable, and we can only hypothesize, in the terms of our theoretical framework, about what they are. The geometrical part of that framework is demonstrable because, says Hobbes, the geometrical shapes which are its objects can be created by ourselves. For the same reasons, political philosophy can be demonstrated. For one thing, the 'motions of our mind', which are the causes of political phenomena, are known directly to us in our experience. For another, the state, or civil society, the object of political philosophy is, like the objects of geometry, of our own creation. In an important passage he writes:

The science of every subject is derived from a precognition of the causes, generation, and construction of the same; and consequently where the causes are known, there is place for demonstration, but not where the causes are to seek for. Geometry therefore is demonstrable, for the lines and figures from which we reason are drawn and described by ourselves; and civil philosophy is demonstrable, because we make the commonwealth ourselves. But because of natural bodies we know not the construction, but seek it from the effects, there lies no demonstration of what the causes be we seek for, but only of what they may be.

In order to understand the state, we need, in accordance with the resolutio-compositive method, first to consider the parts out of which it comes into being. We must look at what people would be like outside of, and prior to, civil society. We must 'consider men as if but even now sprung out of the earth, and suddenly, like mushrooms, come to full maturity, without all kind of engagement to each other'. It does not matter to Hobbes whether men were ever actually in such a 'state of nature', but he suggests that the American Indians are in one somewhat like it.

This is one sense in which we ourselves 'make the commonwealth'. But in fact there are two, for, as Hobbes says, 'we are the *matter* and the *artificer*' of the state. The second sense emerges as we follow his explanation of how the civil state would come into being out of a state of nature, by the making of contracts.

Given Hobbes's view of egocentric human nature, according to which people always act in such a way as to produce pleasure and avoid pain, it is plain how they will behave in an ungoverned state of nature. Living solely by their hopes for what, in effect, will enhance their 'vital motion', and fear of what will impede it, they exist in a state of perpetual fear, suspicion, and competition. In what has become a classic description of this unpleasant and unstable world, in which peaceful planning and long-term effort are pointless, Hobbes says that:

in such a condition, there is no place for industry; because the fruit thereof is uncertain: and consequently no culture of the earth; no navigation, nor use of the commodities that may be imported by sea; no commodious buildings; no instruments of moving, and removing, such things as require much force; no knowledge of the face of the earth; no account of time; no arts; no letters; no society; and which is worst of all, continual fear, and danger of violent death; and the life of man, solitary, poor, nasty, brutish, and short.

In such a state, driven by the worst fear of all, that of sudden death, and given that they are all approximately equal in power, it would seem to be in men's interests that they reach some agreement, each to have only as much liberty as he is prepared to allow to others. But could such an agreement be reached, and would it be kept? A person's real self-interest would lie in *his* not keeping to such an agreement, while others did. But why should others, driven by *their* self-interest, keep the agreement? Trust, as such, is not an element in Hobbesian human nature. 'The dispositions of men are naturally such, that except they be restrained through fear of some coercive power, every man will distrust and dread each other.' What is needed is some mechanism for *enforcement* of the agreement, so that it would be in no one's interest to break it. 'Covenants, without the sword, are but words, and of no strength to secure a man at all.' An agreement is needed, not merely to give up an amount of liberty, but to put it into the hands of some sovereign power. Men need, in effect, to say to each other, 'I authorize and give up my right of governing myself, to this man, or to this assembly of men, on this condition, that they give up their right to him and authorize all his actions in like manner.' From the unlikely beginning of an extreme and unremitting egocentricity, Hobbes has thus explained how it is possible that a civil society can come into being.

Both personally, and in his political philosophy, Hobbes placed a high premium on peace and stability. To some temperaments his state of nature might seem exciting and full of challenge. But from Hobbes's description it seems as though its very contemplation filled him with a trembling, timorous fear. For him, an established and stable state was a necessary condition for the satisfaction of men's desires; the peace it offered was its rationale and justification. This explains the premature publication of *De Cive* in 1642, the year in which mounting resistance to the established monarch, Charles I, resulted in the outbreak of the Civil War. *Leviathan* was published in 1651, two years after Charles was beheaded and Cromwell became Protector of the Commonwealth. Such turmoil, Hobbes thought, arose from ignorance of political and moral science: the cause of civil war is 'that men know not the causes neither of war nor peace'. He claimed to demonstrate these causes. Sovereignty is, and must be, absolute and undivided. The Puritan appeal to individual conscience, the conflicts between Parliament and King, all rest on a misunderstanding of the nature of sovereignty, and its relation to the governed.

Hobbes had left England for Paris in 1640, believing that his political views made this prudent and, as mathematics tutor to the future Charles II, he was associated there with the exiled English court. By 1652 he was back in England where, in the event, he was able to prove acceptable to Parliament. Some said at the time that *Leviathan* had been written for Cromwell, and indeed Hobbes did say that it supported a 'conscientious obedience to the present government' of the Protectorate. Then, finally, in 1662, he apologetically asked Charles II not 'to think the worse of me, if snatching up all the weapons to fight against your enemies, I lighted upon one that had a double edge'. Whatever the complexities of Hobbes's personal motivations, there was no theoretical inconsistency in all of this. He did, indeed, have a marked preference for a monarchy, arguing for it as the 'most commodious government'. But this is, he says, simply a matter of probability. All he claims to have demonstrated is the necessity for some absolute sovereign power or other; according to his theory, this could as easily be a democracy or an aristocracy as a monarchy. Moreover, it follows from this necessity for an absolute sovereign, that an eventual transfer of allegiance is inevitable when the 'sovereign' fails to govern, and keep the civil peace.

In accordance with his political views, Hobbes found no room for religious dissent from an established church with the absolute sovereign as its head. Religious dissent is, indeed, one source of civil unrest. But, although a professed and conforming Anglican, he was often reviled as an atheist. This was largely as a consequence of his undoubted materialism, according to which all that exists is matter in motion. To say that anything spiritual, such as God or the soul, is 'an incorporeal substance, is to say in effect, there is no ... spirit at all'. But, just as Hobbes does not deny we have a mind or soul, so he does not deny the existence of God. Apart, however, from his existence as a corporeal omnipotent first cause, all else about God was a matter of faith.

If the gate of natural philosophy, the ultimate foundation for Hobbes's political philosophy, had been opened by Galileo, others had entered through it along with Harvey. Hobbes mentions Marin Mersenne and Pierre Gassendi as two who had 'extraordinarily advanced' the subject. Hobbes had formed a close friendship with Gassendi during his meetings with him in Paris, in the circle of scientists and philosophers which centred round Mersenne. According to Aubrey, 'they loved each other entirely', and Hobbes never mentioned him 'but with great honour and respect'. He is the subject of the next chapter.

4

Pierre Gassendi (1592-1655)

Pierre Gassendi was born at Champtercier, in the south of France, in 1592. His life was spent in the Church, in teaching, and in private study. A Catholic priest and Canon of Digne, he was also Professor of Philosophy at Aix, and of Mathematics at the Collège Royale in Paris. He was in close contact with many prominent intellectuals and scholars, such as Kepler, Galileo, Hobbes, Descartes, and Mersenne, and was very highly regarded both inside and outside France, where he lived until his death in 1655. His writings, with their discussions of the nature of science, contain the basis of a theoretical empiricism. But he was also interested in the substantial factual detail of astronomy, anatomy, and the physics of motion. He made, and published, many observations on these matters, having been persuaded by Snell, the celebrated Dutch mathematician, that there was some point in studying nature as well as books. He was a vegetarian and teetotaller and, in Hobbes's view (so Aubrey tells us), 'the sweetest-natured man in the world'. Only controversy with Descartes was able to disturb his mildness.

Despite his fame amongst his contemporaries, Gassendi has been overshadowed by those whom he influenced—perhaps because of the modesty and undogmatic nature of his arguments, which lie buried in lengthy, copiously annotated Latin works. An English summary of some of these appeared in 1654, and François Bernier produced a famous French abridgement between 1674 and 1678. But some of his work is still not available in modern French, and most of it not in English. He is best known now for his *Objections* (1644) to Descartes's *Meditations*, which are remarkable for the vituperative annoyance which runs through them. Although they constitute a thorough attack on Descartes's rationalism, Gassendi's empiricism is developed elsewhere.

Chapter 1 has described how one of the movements in seventeenth-century thought was the rejection of scholastic philosophy in general, and its account of scientific explanation in particular. The rejection of the theory of hylemorphism, according to which natural phenomena and the properties of things are to be understood in terms of form and matter, is implicit in Bacon. Though he spoke of 'forms' as the explanatory factors in things, his conception of them differs, as we saw, from that of the Aristotelians. The rejection is there in Hobbes too; for him the basis of explanation is matter in motion. The picture of the universe as a mechanical affair of matter in motion did not originate, but rather was painted afresh, in the seventeenth century; it was derived from the atomic theory of the ancient Greeks, Democritus and Epicurus. But as dissatisfaction with scholastic theory increased, so did acceptance of ancient atomism, and Gassendi has a prime responsibility for its revival.

According to Gassendi's own report, he was dissatisfied from the start with the Aristotelianism he was taught as a student. He quickly discovered, however, that other schools of philosophy, despite proud boasts to the contrary, had nothing better to offer. Consequently, in a spirit of scepticism, he came to distrust all dogmatic claims to knowledge. The unsatisfactoriness of the competing claims of various philosophers first led him to the belief that scientific knowledge of nature was unattainable by the human mind. Unlike Bacon, who supposed that his method of inquiry would give certainty, he concluded that judgement on such matters ought to be suspended. It was possible to see both good and bad in any view, and this proved 'the vanity as well as the uncertainty of human knowledge'. Gassendi thus provides a notable example of the influence of the rediscovery in the sixteenth century of Sextus Empiricus' *Outlines of Pyrrhonism*, to which reference has already been made. The markedly sceptical attitude and arguments which run through his writings are derived from Sextus, and from others, such as Michel Montaigne and Pierre Charron, who were themselves influenced by Sextus.

Even though he was dissatisfied with Aristotle's teachings, Gassendi was required, as professor of philosophy, to expound them to his students, just as his own professors had expounded them to him. He dutifully did this. But by way of indicating that they were not, and could not be, the final truth, he appended a series of objections to his lecture course. Shortly after leaving Aix he published them as *Exercises in the Form of Paradoxes against the Aristotelians* (1624). The whole tone of these is somewhat scathing. Indeed, Gassendi acknowledges that 'in this matter it is especially difficult not to write satirically'. Though immensely enjoyable to read, the *Exercises* give no impression that Gassendi is doing the best by his opponents before attacking them. Of course, much of that would have been done in his lectures, to which the anti-Aristotelian *Exercises* are an appendix. He does go some way towards outlining counter-arguments and replies, but his style is the playful one of a cat with a mouse.

His initial general complaints about the whole tenor, style, and intellectual bent of the Aristotelians are of the common seventeenth-century sort, which were outlined in Chapter 1. They are there in Bacon, and in Hobbes, and they are there again in Locke. The Aristotelians are conservative and obstructive to the progress of philosophy and knowledge. They go in for querulous and disputatious argument. Their real interest is in point-scoring and success in debate, not in the advancement of genuine knowledge. They focus on words and arguments, not on real things and observations. They look too much to the past, and have an undue reliance on the words and works of their master Aristotle. They think that all knowledge is to be found by perusing him, and not by looking at the real world. They comment on, gloss, and interpret his writings, and spend too little time in empirical observation and investigation. In common with Bacon, Gassendi does not say that Aristotle is completely valueless: he acknowledges the greatness of his mind. His criticisms are directed more at his followers, who fail to recognize, not only that other great past minds have something to teach, but also, more importantly, that there could be great minds in the future. These, perhaps by building on parts of Aristotle, will be able to advance knowledge even further than he did.

Gassendi's criticisms are not all of this general sort, however. He launches a detailed attack on the many aspects of scholastic teaching which had their basis in the logical works of Aristotle's

Organon. One of these is its account of what *scientia*, or an organized body of knowledge, is like. Though our more recent notion of a developed science, such as physics or chemistry, is directly descended from this, our conception of how such sciences come about, and the methods of investigation appropriate to them, differs in certain important respects from that of the Aristotelians. In large measure, these differences are due to the criticisms of the Aristotelian scheme made by some of those who are treated in this book, and in its companion, *The Rationalists*.

According to the Aristotelian picture, *scientia*, or knowledge proper, is knowledge of what is necessary and cannot be otherwise. Strictly speaking, there can be no 'knowledge' of things that are so, but that could have been otherwise. What was called 'opinion' has to do with contingent facts of this sort. To have such 'scientific knowledge' of, say, the facts that man is the only animal with a sense of humour, that gold dissolves in *aqua regia*, or that triangles have angles equal to two right angles, is to know that these things must be so and cannot be otherwise. And this involves having a demonstrative understanding of the causes why these things have these properties. In general terms, Bacon and Hobbes accept the Aristotelian idea that scientific understanding involves knowledge of causes. Gassendi accepts it too. But, in a more explicit and forceful way, he objects to the particular account of such knowledge in which this general idea was embedded by Aristotle and his scholastic followers.

To demonstrate that something necessarily has a certain property, so the theory runs, is to show, by means of a syllogistic argument from certain axioms or first principles, that it has it. The logical theory of syllogistic arguments was developed in great detail by Aristotle, and survives to this day in introductory logic textbooks. In itself, there is nothing wrong with it. What was wrong was the scholastic insistence that all arguments, all reasoning, could, and should, be put into this form. In particular, what was wrong was their idea that 'science' should consist of demonstrative syllogisms, and their view of what the premisses of these should be like.

According to this account, to serve as satisfactory starting-points for scientific demonstration, the first principles, or axioms, need themselves to be indemonstrable; otherwise a demonstration would be needed of them. They need to be 'better known to nature' too, prior in the order of things to the conclusions established on their basis. If they were not, then, as we saw in the echoes of this theory which can be found in Hobbes's resolutio-compositive method, the proper order of demonstration would have been reversed. They are of two sorts. Some are things that have to be known if anything at all is to be known. Common examples are general principles of reasoning, such as the law of non-contradiction (that nothing can both be and not be), and the proposition that, if equals are taken from equals, then equals remain. Others are special to the subject-matter under consideration. They pick that subject out and define it. As the English word 'science' might lead us to expect, *scientia* falls into various bodies of knowledge, or sciences, distinguished by their different subject-matters. Each science has to do with its own genus, or 'kind', which is divided by 'differentia' into various species. Geometry deals with plane figures such as triangles and squares. Similarly, biology has as its subject the genus 'animal', a genus which falls into various species such as 'dog' or 'horse'. Each science needs to be prefaced by an account, or definition in terms of genus and differentia, of the various species with which it deals. A syllogism with premisses of this sort gives a demonstrative understanding of the causes why things necessarily have the properties they do, because the definitions with which it starts are definitions of the 'forms' of these things, and formal causes are one of the four kinds of cause which Aristotle distinguished.

According to the hylemorphic theory of the scholastics, each individual thing or substance is a combination of 'matter' (*hyle*) and 'form' (*morphe*), and it is because something has the form it has, that it is the kind of thing it is. The definition of the species 'man' is supposed to give a real definition of man, an account of his 'form', 'essence', 'nature', or 'substantial form'. 'Definition', Aristotle says, 'reveals essential nature.' But besides 'natures', 'essences', or 'substantial forms' of the various genera and species, there are properties which members of that species universally and permanently have, and it is the aim of 'science' to tell us why they have them. Though all triangles have angles equal to two right angles, having this is no part of their essence or definition. The complete essence or form of a triangle is to be a three-sided plane figure. Nevertheless, even though having angles equal to two right angles is not part of a triangle's essence, it is because it is a three-sided plane figure that it has them. Properties of this sort were supposed to 'flow', 'derive', or 'emanate' from the form. As Aquinas says, 'a thing's characteristic operations derive from its substantial form'. The essence, or form, of a species accounts for the properties of that species, and a definition of it provides the means of demonstrating that the species does have those properties, and why it has them. Facts about the properties of a given species are exactly the facts that a 'science', with its initial definitions, is meant to give causal knowledge of. Science is knowledge of what is necessarily the case, and of why it is so. The properties of a species necessarily belong to things of that kind, and the essence, or definition, of that species is the cause, or reason, for their having them. So one has acquired scientific knowledge when one has a series of syllogisms which, on the basis of 'formal' definitions and other first principles, demonstrates that certain properties of a species must belong to it. Just as essences or forms give rise to those properties, so definitions of those forms, when used as premisses, give rise to conclusions about those properties. *Scientia*, or scientific knowledge, consists of syllogisms such that the derivation of conclusions from their premisses mirrors the 'flowing' of properties from forms. This theory was backed up by an elaborate logical system which gave strict rules for the production of unambiguous definitions of species in terms of their genus and their difference from other related species, and for the validity and relevance of syllogisms.

Along with others, Gassendi obviously felt that this whole elaborate conceptual structure was obstructive to, rather than productive of, knowledge. It too easily degenerated into a concern with trivial verbal classifications, and artificial categories. To begin with, we have no need, he argues, of Aristotelian logic, and are not helped by it. We have no need formally to be told to avoid ambiguities. Anyone with a desire for truth will unreflectingly and instinctively do this. The rules of an artificial formal logic will not guide one in the search for the natures of things.

Just what routes will logic produce to lead me to the complete knowledge of the nature of a flea? ... Is it truly the province of logic to examine, to uncover, and consequently to explain the nature of things, rather than the province of Physics and the other sciences instead? What olfactory sense is logic endowed with that it sniffs out and runs to ground the hidden nature of things?

Anyone trying to understand something will naturally compare it with other things to find similarities and differences. No one thinks explicitly in terms of genus and differentia, and the scholastic rules for definitions. No one is helped by doing so, or by reporting his discoveries in a tortured, tidied-up, formal account. The Aristotelian talk of definitions 'does not reveal nature to us, but only does the same as the man who promised to discover a treasure and then says "look where it is hidden and you will find it."'

Not only are we not helped by scholastic logic to acquire knowledge of the forms, natures, or essences of things, and to see how other properties flow from them, but also it is extremely doubtful whether such knowledge is possible anyway. We just do not know the natures we are supposed to know, or how various properties follow from them. What is the 'essence' or 'nature' of a horse, and why does it follow from this that a horse has a certain type of head or feet, or lives to the age it does? What is the 'form' of a flea, and will it explain its ability to digest blood, and to move with agility? 'What qualities result from that form deep within him, and how?' 'Rational animal' had been suggested as a definition of the 'nature' of man; but this appears to be no more than a specification of some of his properties. The formal definitions of the Aristotelians are either unattainable, or hardly serve their intended purpose.

Even ignoring the fact that they were meant as definitions of natures or essences, Gassendi finds something wrong with the idea of finding universal propositions for the premises of a scientific syllogism. It is doubtful that universal propositions of any sort can be got. Unless we perform the impossibility of checking all their instances, they always risk falsification by one counter-instance. 'You will surely tell me that this universal proposition is true "Every man is a biped" ... And yet if I refer you to no other example than that little one-legged girl whom we saw not so long ago in our Provence, doesn't your universal statement collapse?'

There is a good illustration here of how Gassendi's attacks do not take his opponents as seriously as might be. It was not, for them, simply a matter of supposing that what held true in some cases would hold in all, but of their coming to see a particular case as an instance of an intuitively recognizable universal truth. One need not mechanically check a large number of triangles to see that some of what holds of one will hold of all. He is too quick, moreover, in his offhand dismissal of the thought that the girl was 'abnormal': 'You may say whatever you want; still it is enough to make your universal declaration false if one single case contradicts you.' The unsympathetic nature of his criticisms is also illustrated by what he says about the requirement that such universal premises be 'better known' than their conclusions. That all men laugh is supposed to be demonstrated from the premises that all men are rational and that all rational things laugh. But surely, says Gassendi, it is 'better known' that all men laugh than that all rational beings do. As we saw in connection with Hobbes's method, however, the traditional idea was not, as Gassendi chooses to suppose, that a demonstrated conclusion should be 'more known' *to us*, or first in the order of knowledge. It was that it should be 'more known' *to nature*, first in the order of things.

Finally, Gassendi attacks the idea that proofs must be syllogistic in form. Even Aristotle's own practice contradicts this. 'Indeed, if Aristotle was a master of the art and handed his philosophy down to us very carefully, shouldn't he have proven everything in the most perfect form, especially when he insisted upon it himself—unless perhaps he intended to make fun of us?'

Running through Gassendi's forthright rejection of the Aristotelian apparatus of definitions of 'forms' and syllogistic demonstration of scientific knowledge, is something more positive. He frequently implies that knowledge is to be had by experience and by careful observation of the world. Farmers, sailors, and chemists get by perfectly well on the basis of everyday experience, without recourse to Aristotelian logic. If anything can help us uncover the natures of things, it is not logic, but physics, and the other observational sciences. If there is an 'in-strument' of scientific knowledge, it is not the content of Aristotle's *Organon*, but 'painstaking experience'. Logic does not provide the means of distinguishing the true from the false. 'Experience is the balance in which the truth of any matter is to be weighed, such as whether fire is hot or not, whether the sun is bright or dim.'

But we must not build too much, at this early stage in Gassendi's thought, on these positive aspects of it. We should remember that he does not claim definitely to be refuting the Aristotelians, but merely to be pointing out what may be said against them. His aim is not to show that one way of acquiring knowledge is better than another, but that 'learning and human knowledge are weak and uncertain'. I cannot, he says, 'really persuade myself that the truth of things can be perceived by mortal men'. So, even though he continually contrasts the value of everyday experience with the emptiness of Aristotelian procedures, he in fact goes on to argue that everyday experience also is powerless to give us knowledge of the nature of things.

The arguments he uses here are standard ones, taken over bodily from the ten 'tropes' of the Greek sceptics as presented in Diogenes Laertius' *Life of Pyrrho*, and Sextus Empiricus' *Outlines of Pyrrhonism*. They purport to show that judgement should be suspended on all matters. There are many things that 'our experience shows us ... by the testimony of the senses'; for example 'that fire is hot and tends upwards, that water is cold and flows downhill, that honey is sweet'. But there is reason to think that our senses do not take us to the heart of things. To mention only the first 'trope', there are great differences between animals, in the manner of their birth, their way of life, their physical constitution, and so on. Consequently 'they have senses that are affected in different ways', and perceive things differently.

So Gassendi pursues two lines of thought in his *Exercises against the Aristotelians*. On the one hand, he rejects the idea that we can attain knowledge in the form of demonstrative understanding that certain things must be so, an understanding based on knowledge of the real natures or essences of things. Aristotelian logic does not provide any basis for such knowledge.

On the other hand, he argues that knowledge of 'inner natures or necessary causes' is not attainable on the basis of sense-experience either. As a consequence, 'it becomes apparent', he says, 'that no proposition that makes assertions about the nature of a thing according to itself can be affirmed with confidence.' This is so not only in physics, but also in mathematics, which, we might have supposed, does provide knowledge of the real natures of numbers and geometrical figures, and demonstrations about the causes of their properties. A mathematical proof about some property of a triangle does not, Gassendi thinks, give demonstrative understanding of its cause. It merely reveals that the triangle does indeed have it. 'When a mathematician proves some proposition you had not known, he accomplishes no more than a man who discloses the contents of a casket ... by opening it up.'

But there is more to Gassendi's final position in his *Exercises* than this. Undoubtedly he has argued that on *no* account is knowledge of necessary causes or real inner natures possible. Neither Aristotelian logic nor sense-experience can get us it. But does this mean that *no* knowledge is possible? Are the sceptics right in saying *nihil sciri*, that nothing can be known? If knowledge, properly speaking, is knowledge of necessary causes, or real inner natures, then they are. But is knowledge like this? Might not what we acquire on the basis of sense-experience, knowledge of the appearances of things, count as knowledge? If so, then where the Aristotelians go wrong is not so much that their procedures do not get us knowledge, as that they have a restricted or incorrect notion of what knowledge actually is. Of course, the same fault should then be laid at the sceptics' door. In saying that our senses restrict us to appearances and that therefore we know nothing, they would mistakenly be supposing that knowledge is exclusively knowledge of necessary causes and inner natures. They would have failed to recognize and acknowledge that what we have on the basis of sense-experience is worth having, and worthy of the name of knowledge.

Gassendi shows some tendency to endorse this line of thought. He hints that it would be wrong to 'persist in regarding knowledge as the certain and evident cognition of a thing, obtained through an acquaintance with its necessary cause, or by a proof ', for then 'knowledge through experience or appearances would not merit the name of knowledge'. Perhaps one should 'allow that a certain knowledge derived from our experience of the appearances of things should be termed genuine knowledge'. He himself, he says, does 'not belong to the party that would condemn the common and familiar ways of speaking', according to which we know many things at the level of appearances, such as that I am now seated rather than standing, and that fire appears hot rather than cold. So, despite his presentation of sceptical arguments against knowledge of the nature of things, Gassendi does, nevertheless, hint that 'it may well be that the basis for knowledge does exist'; even though this will be 'a knowledge of experience and, I may say, of appearances'. It can still be said, he suggests, 'that there are some things capable of being known, though they are still not ones that can be known with an Aristotelian knowledge, but only experientially, or according to appearances'.

There is a hint of something else, too, when he considers the suggestion that, even though the senses take us no further than appearances, perhaps the understanding can penetrate further to the inner natures of things. Of course, he denies that it can. But he expresses this by saying that we 'can proceed no farther by reasoning than to things which must be exposed again to experience or which can be evidenced by means of some appearance'; and this seems to suggest something new. It seems to allow that, although we must begin and end with appearances, we might find it possible and advantageous in doing so to interpose conjectures about their hidden causes.

But, so far as the *Exercises* goes, all of this is underplayed. Gassendi does not develop the thought that 'the labours of the most outstanding philosophers ... need not be considered useless just because they have not produced an Aristotelian knowledge for us so far; for they have produced another sort which is more true and useful, namely knowledge from experience and the appearance of things.' Nor does he flesh out the suggestion of improving and extending our knowledge of appearances through the mediation of hypothetical conjectures about hidden causes, causes which are 'evidenced' by appearances. We must turn to Gassendi's later work, the *Syntagma Philosophicum* ('Philosophical Treatise') for a more confident development of these ideas.

The *Syntagma* grew out of an interest Gassendi formed, not long after the publication of the *Exercises*, in the Greek philosopher Epicurus. The *Exercises* were ill-received, and Gassendi seems to have decided that he might make more headway against the Aristotelians by systematically presenting an alternative point of view, rather than by direct argument against them. His initial intention was to publish something on Epicurus merely as an appendix to the *Exercises*. But his interest grew as he worked, and he began to aim at a comprehensive expository commentary on Epicurus. The eventual result was the posthumous publication, in 1658, of the *Syntagma*, which uses the medium of a commentary on Epicurus as a vehicle for an account of Gassendi's own thought.

For some centuries now, an 'epicure' has been someone overly devoted to sensual pleasure and luxury. Epicurus did, indeed, place supreme value on 'pleasure'; but he thought of this as the calm tranquillity and freedom from anxiety which would be achieved by realizing that there is no life after death, and that we are not subject to outside divine influences. Epicurus taught, therefore, a thoroughgoing materialism according to which our world is simply the chance production of atoms coming together in their fall through an infinite void. There are gods, but they too are only material combinations of atoms, and our own consciousness ceases at death on the disintegration of our material bodies. Such a picture—derived essentially from the earlier atomist Democritus—may seem bleak to some, but to Epicurus and his followers it was productive of the calm *ataraxia* he valued. Epicurus' influence on Gassendi relates to his taking pleasure and pain as the measure of what is good, and sense-experience as the criterion, or measure, of truth. As for the first, it should be remembered that for an Epicurean the worst pain is the groundless fear of what may happen after death, and that excessive unnatural desires are painful too. As for truth, Epicurus, rather like Hobbes centuries later, took sense-perception to be simply the effect of objects on our material souls. Accordingly, our sensations simply are as they are, and error enters only when we make mistaken judgements on their basis. A distant square tower really does look round; any mistake lies in judging that it *is* round, and can be corrected by further sense-experience. Not only did Gassendi take sense-experience to be the criterion or measure of truth, he also adopted Epicurus' atomistic view of the universe.

In studying Epicurus, Gassendi found confirmation for the embryonic idea of the *Exercises*, that sense-experience might give us something worthwhile and valuable even though it cannot give us knowledge of necessary causes and of the natures of things. More and more, he saw importance in experience. Perhaps it is not as useless as Aristotelian logic and can lead, if not to knowledge of necessary causes and natures, then to something worthwhile nevertheless. This development in his thought coincided with an ever-increasing interest in detailed, experimental, physical matters.

Gassendi begins by addressing a question first raised by the Greek sceptics, as we saw in Chapter 1. Is there such a thing as a 'criterion' of truth? Do we have any 'instrument' or means of getting at the truth? The traditional choice, which Gassendi outlines, was between the senses on the one hand, and the mind, understanding, or reason on the other. Against their opponents, the dogmatics, the sceptics had argued, by means of their 'tropes' or 'modes', that neither sense-experience nor intellectual thought can be a 'criterion' or 'instrument' of truth. Though this, in effect, had been Gassendi's official position in the *Exercises*, he now hopes to find a way between the dogmatics and the sceptics. He hopes to show that, although we cannot know quite what the former say we can, nevertheless we can still know more than the latter allow.

With this aim in view, he makes explicit that what the sceptics deny is the possibility of knowledge of 'the inner nature of things ... what the things are in themselves'; when they say that there is no criterion of truth, 'they are not speaking of what things appear to be and of what is revealed by the senses ... but of what things are in themselves, which is so hidden that no criterion can disclose it'. Given this, we must recognize that knowledge of appearances is not, in itself, such a worthless thing; what we know on the basis of sense-experience is perfectly good for many purposes. Even if

we cannot get at 'the truth itself' and 'be admitted into the very
inner shrines of nature', we can at least 'glimpse ... some slight
image of it', and 'live among certain of the outer altars'. It is
absurd to 'yearn to fly like the birds' when we have feet to get us
where we want to go. Furthermore, and perhaps more importantly from the point of view of answering the sceptics, even
though we cannot directly get at the hidden real natures of things,
perhaps our knowledge of appearances will enable us to do so
indirectly. 'The truth in question is hidden, lying concealed be-
neath appearances; we must then inquire, since its nature is not
open to us, whether it is still possible to know it through some
sign and whether we have a criterion by which we may recognize
the sign and judge what the thing truly is.'

In his elaboration of this suggestion, whose seeds were already
present in the *Exercises*, Gassendi draws on classical Greek
thought, according to which there are three sorts of 'hidden' thing.
Some things, such as whether the number of stars is odd or even,
are totally hidden; we shall never, could never, come to know the
truth about that. Others are merely temporarily hidden, such as
whether there is fire behind a building which obstructs our line of
sight; we could come to know about this by going to see. But the
notion of things which are naturally hidden is most important
for Gassendi. Unlike temporarily hidden things, these cannot
'become evident by their own nature', but we can 'nevertheless
know and understand [them] through something else'. The pores
in the skin are a classic example: they 'cannot become perceptible
to us by themselves, but yet their presence in the skin can be
deduced from sweat'.

The sceptics did not deny that by means of what was traditionally called an 'empirical' sign we might be led to indirect
knowledge of something temporarily hidden: smoke from over
the building is a sign that there is a fire behind. What they did
deny were 'indicative' signs, by which we could be led to indirect
knowledge of something naturally hidden, such as pores in the
skin. Gassendi says they were simply wrong about this. The
existence of such pores is undoubtedly hidden from us, 'for pores
cannot be seen'. Nevertheless, 'sweat is of such a nature that it
would not appear upon the skin unless pores existed through

which it could pass from inside to the outside'. There simply are such 'indicative' signs, and they are presented to us in sense-experience; on their basis we can reason to the hidden things which they 'indicate'.

What, then, of the arguments of the sceptics that we cannot claim knowledge about reality? Gassendi accepts them, but draws their sting. It is, indeed, true that all that is manifest to us is appearances. However, such knowledge is, in itself, no useless thing. Again, even though things do appear differently to different people, this is due to differences in the people, not to there being no reality behind the appearances. It is the same heat in the sun that melts wax and hardens clay, and it is possible, perhaps by the use of indicative signs, to investigate the underlying causes of dissimilar effects. If someone should succeed in doing this in some particular case, says Gassendi,

he will be considered to have nothing less than full acquaintance with the nature of the thing and to share in the knowledge of it. For no matter how much it is objected that it cannot be stated definitely from these considerations just what the thing is like according to its nature, but only what it is like in respect to one thing or to another, it may still be said what there is in it which makes it appear to be this in respect to one thing and that in respect to another; and consequently it may be said both to be one thing according to its nature and to be this or that in respect to other things.

In general terms, Gassendi's notion of such 'hidden things' or 'natures' is entirely in accordance with tradition and the contemporary usage of his time. It is 'the underlying component of all properties, faculties, and operations' of some thing. It is the 'underground spring, so to speak' of the properties of a thing which are known to us by our senses. According to the Aristotelians, the nature of a thing is, specifically, its 'substantial form' as explained in their hylemorphic theory. As we saw earlier, in this and the first chapter, this theory holds that things are a combination of form and matter, and it is by appeal to their form that one would hope to explain why things have the properties they do. Gassendi's suspicion of the Aristotelian account is evident from his *Exercises*, and his study of Epicurean philosophy provided him with an alternative. The atomic theory suggests a different picture of the nature of matter, and a different form of explanation from that given by hylemorphism. Gassendi adopted it enthusiastically and argued for it at great length. According to it, the properties of things are to be explained and accounted for, not in terms of real definitions of their forms, but by reference to the atoms which make them up. A thing's properties, and its actions and reactions on other things, are understood instead in terms of the shapes, sizes, motions, and consequent mechanical reactions of its atomic constitution and make-up. Just as his theoretical awareness of the importance of sense-experience as a basis for science went along with an increasing interest in practical, experimental investigation of the world, so his theoretical advocacy of Epicurean atomism went along with his actual use of it in his own work; for example, in an account he gave of various optical phenomena produced by the sun.

Gassendi does not claim, of course, that it is any more than a hypothesis that the properties, changes, and actions of things are to be explained by reference to their atomic parts. The idea that they are is not supported by our immediate experience. But it is, he thinks, more plausible, intelligible, and fruitful than any other. In this he had the agreement of the 'new philosophers' of his century. The increasing popularity of a broadly corpuscularian or atomistic approach to explanation is largely due to Gassendi's endeavours on its behalf.

Despite its attractions as the basis for scientific explanation, classical atomism had the drawback of having its roots in Epicurus' materialistic atheism. For this reason, the seventeenth century looked on it with varying degrees of embarrassed caution and suspicion. As a Catholic priest, Gassendi believed in God and the immortality of an immaterial soul. His adoption of classical atomism was, consequently, not a wholesale one, and he made various changes in its basic principles. Rather than being eternal and having motion because of their fall through the void, the atoms are, for Gassendi, created and directed in their motion by God. Finite in number, the limited material world they make up is not all there is, for, besides an infinite God, we have immaterial souls. He was sympathetic to the Epicurean ideal of a tranquil mind. He believed that the study of nature was conducive to this, but he rejected the connection of this ideal with atheism. The fact that we could only hypothesize via 'indicative' signs about the natures of things should not lead to discontent. There are things which God has not given us to know, and we must learn to accept this patiently.

Gassendi has argued that, despite what the sceptics say, it is possible, by inferring back, to arrive at some truth about hidden things. It is, he says, the province of physics and the other sciences to seek the truth in their own areas. But logic, which he defines as the 'art of clear thinking', can provide 'general precepts and rules, common to all branches, of learning. 'Clear thinking' falls into four parts, 'forming clear ideas, stating propositions clearly, making clear deductions, organizing thought clearly.' We will not follow Gassendi in much of this, but it will be of interest to note what he says in so far as it relates to experience.

On the forming of clear ideas, Gassendi has some good words to say about Bacon. He praises him for insisting that we free ourselves from the Idols, get rid of preconceived notions, and form our ideas on the basis of properly conducted experiments. He praises him too for his advocacy of careful and methodical procedures based on careful consideration of individual cases. Much of what Gassendi says about the acquisition and formation of ideas became commonplace among later empiricists, being developed by Locke in more detail and at much greater length. 'Every idea which is held in the mind takes its origin from the senses ... [it] either comes through the senses, or is formed from those which come through the senses.' All our ideas are derived from experience, and he argues, against Descartes, that there are no innate ideas which are with us at birth. A blind man lacks the ideas of colour because he lacks the requisite experience, and a man 'deprived of every sense ... would have no idea of a single thing'. But the acquisition of ideas from experience is not a straightforwardly passive matter. We can have ideas of things we have not experienced. We can form the idea of a golden mountain, or of a centaur, by combining and adapting others we already have from experience. On the same basis, we can get ideas from descriptions given to us by others. Similarly, although anything that exists is particular and individual, we can have general ideas.

On the basis of our ideas of particular men, we can form a general idea of 'man', and by abstracting differences from the ideas of 'man', 'horse', and 'lion', we can form still more general ideas, such as that of 'animal'.

The fourth part of Gassendi's Logic has to do with the organization of thought, or *method*. In accordance with the traditional scheme, he distinguishes methods of investigation and discovery from methods of teaching, and refers to the old notions of analysis and resolution, composition and synthesis. Discoveries need to be checked, of course, so Gassendi adds the method of judgement or assessment. This too uses analysis and synthesis: analysis if the discovery to be checked has been made by synthesis, synthesis if it was made by analysis. As he remarks, this is what we do in arithmetic when we check additions by subtraction, and vice versa.

Though Gassendi followed Epicurus in taking sense-experience as the criterion, or measure, of truth, and that on which our judgements should be based, he combines this criterion with its traditional rival, reason. Though all our knowledge 'is in the senses or derived from them', it is not always simply a matter of sensory information. 'The senses ... ultimately provide the material', but reason, or 'the innate force and power of the understanding', has its place too. There are cases where the senses are sufficient. As Gassendi insists in his *Objections* to Descartes, there is no need forever to be distrustful of them. Judgements based on the senses often are incorrect; but, as Epicurus noted, they can be corrected by further appeal to the same authority. A tower may seem round from a distance, but there is no need to doubt our closer observation that it is square. Sometimes, moreover, experience can show that our reasoning is superficial and incorrect, as when we learn from it that, despite what we might think, an arrow fired upwards from a moving ship will not fall behind but back on to it. At other times, however, reason can correct the appearances of sense; from the waxing and waning of the moon, according to how it is illuminated by the sun, we can deduce that it is a globe, and not the flat disc it appears to be. Furthermore, as when we infer from observed sweat the existence of pores in the skin, reason can lead us from what can be perceived to what cannot.

Gassendi's empiricist views on the derivation of our ideas from sense-experience, on natural philosophy and its foundation in carefully considered observation, and his stress on the explanatory value of Epicurean atomism, were already well known to Hobbes and others when they were formally introduced into England via the publication, in 1654, of Walter Charleton's *Physiologia Epicuro-gassendo-Charltonia: a Fabrick of Science Natural upon the Hypothesis of Atoms, Founded by Epicurus, Repaired by Petrus Gassendus, Augmented by Walter Charleton.* Charleton was involved from its early days with the subject of the next chapter, The Royal Society of London for the Improving of Natural Knowledge.

5
The Royal Society of London for the Improving of Natural Knowledge (1660–)

In Chapter 1, and along the way, we have seen how a characteristic feature of seventeenth-century thought was its anti-Aristotelianism. In general, the Aristotelians were thought to lay too much stress on words and books, terminology and merely verbal classifications, and debate and controversy, and too little on things and observation of the world. More specifically, the scholastic conception of *scientia*, or scientific knowledge, was thought to be an inappropriate model for empirical knowledge of nature. Particularly in connection with Bacon and Gassendi, we have seen how, in opposition to it, there began to develop a conception of 'natural philosophy'; a body of knowledge based firmly on the experienced facts of experiment and observation, rather than on the intellectual strait-jacket of the logic and categories of Aristotelianism.

It needs to be stressed, what this chapter may serve to illustrate, that developments of this sort should not simply be identified with a few individual thinkers. Noteworthy individuals, such as Bacon, Hobbes, or Gassendi, are not isolated mountains in a flat desert landscape. They have an influence on an intellectual scene which encompasses a whole host of lesser thinkers, and they act as focuses for movements of thought which find powerful expression in them before passing on, often changed, or with added force.

The anti-Aristotelianism and the newly emerging concept of natural philosophy were, then, not private but public developments. So much is this the case that, in the mid-seventeenth century, they came together in a formally institutionalized way in the founding of the Royal Society of London for the Improving of Natural Knowledge. This, along with parallel societies in other European countries, was a tangible and conspicuous product of the anti-traditionalism of the period. Moreover, just as natural science as we know it today is, to an important extent, a product of seventeenth-century philosophical ideas, so one of the pillars of the orthodox scientific establishment in England now is the Royal Society. To be elected a Fellow, or FRS, is a mark of the highest prestige.

The Royal Society had its early beginnings in informal meetings and discussion groups, and became properly institutionalized in the 1660s, shortly before receiving Charters from Charles II. On the list of its early members are such notable names as Robert Boyle, popularly remembered now for his work on the expansion of gases, Christopher Wren, the architect of St Paul's Cathedral, John Evelyn, the diarist, John Locke (who will be the subject of the next chapter of this book), Robert Hooke, remembered now for his work on elasticity, and, perhaps the most famous of all, Isaac Newton.

Not long after its foundation, Thomas Sprat was commissioned to write the Society's *History*. The prefatory ode, by the poet Abraham Cowley, relates how philosophy has been 'kept in non-age' by people who, jealous of their authority, concentrated on words rather than on things, on 'sports of wanton wit', on 'pageants of the brain', rather than on 'the riches which do hoorded lye in Natures endless treasurie'. Throughout the *History*, and other writings of the period, are scathing references to traditional teaching, in particular to that of the Aristotelians. The very motto of the Society, '*Nullius in Verba*' ('In the words of no one else'), encapsulates this general rejection of the authority of the past.

Even if they were sufficiently eminent, not all of the members of the Royal Society would have a place in the History of Science as we might think of it now. There was no expectation then, as there is now, that an FRS would have made any distinctive and weighty contribution to the experimental or theoretical sciences. It has been estimated that, in its early days, only about one third of Royal Society Fellows were scientists. The interest of the rest of the 'virtuosi' (as they were known) was a more general one in the 'new philosophy' and its aims; for the fact is that the Royal Society provided a focus for a whole movement of thought. Though modern empirical experimental science is one of the more obvious products of that movement, the Society was not narrowly restricted to science in any modern sense. It was more broadly philosophical, and encapsulated a generalized dissatisfaction with scholasticism and tradition.

It must be realized, moreover, that there is a hidden complexity to the apparently simple fact that the natural science of later centuries is a product of that time. It is not as though there always was a clear conception of what such a science would be like, and as though all that was lacking was success in producing it. It is, rather, that the very idea of a body of knowledge about the world, of the sort we have now, the very idea of a natural science, was being forged at the time. As we have seen, *scientia*, or scientific knowledge as the seventeenth century understood it, was not something which could be obtained from an observation-based study of the natural world. Even when such a study became established, with worked-out conceptual underpinning, it was not called 'natural science', but 'natural philosophy'. Science, as the seventeenth century traditionally understood it, was not something that could result from activities of the sort advocated by the Royal Society. This meant that the new 'natural philosophy' stood in need, not merely of practical development, but also of intellectual justification and explanation. Not merely science, but also the *idea* of science, was at issue. It is, of course, precisely the concern with such matters, the concern with 'method' and the nature of 'natural philosophy' that has often been the topic of discussion in previous chapters.

The frontispiece of Sprat's *History* shows a spacious study lined with books and scientific instruments. Beyond can be seen the outside world of 'Natures endless treasurie', with a telescope trained on the heavens. In the room, Fame places a wreath on a bust of Charles II, which is flanked by two people. One is Lord Brounker, then President of the Society. The other is Francis Bacon, with the title '*Artium Instaurator*' ('Instigator of Skills'). One could imagine the room to be one in Bacon's House of Solomon, about which Joseph Glanvill remarked that it was 'a prophetic scheme of the Royal Society'. The influence of Bacon on the Royal Society is frequently testified to by its members. Sprat says that he 'had the true imagination of the whole extent of this enterprise, as it is now set on foot'.

We should take this to refer not only to Bacon's schemes for collaboration in natural philosophy, schemes actually embodied in the existence of the Royal Society, but also to his very conception of that subject. Abraham Cowley compares Bacon to Moses, leading the way through a barren wilderness bereft of knowledge, and pointing out the promised land. In Bacon's books, Sprat says, 'are every where scattered the best arguments, that can be produced for the defence of Experimental Philosophy; and the best directions, that are needful to promote it', while according to Glanvill 'all the main heads of natural history have received aids and increase from the famous Bacon, who led the way to substantial wisdom, and hath given most excellent directions for the method of such an history of nature'. Boyle refers to him again and again, 'one of the first and greatest experimental philosophers of our age'.

According to Sprat, then, and others of the Society, knowledge was to be had by turning away from the teachings of the scholastics, from their undue concentration on words, to the world itself. This meant, first and foremost, following Bacon in the making of natural histories. They were to be the basis of a new natural philosophy, and were advocated both by practising experimenters and by theoreticians. Robert Hooke urges in his *Micrographia* that 'the science of nature has already too long been made only a work of the brain and fancy: It is now high time that it should return to the plainness and soundness of observations on material and obvious things.' Henry Power speaks of the need to 'lay a new foundation of a more magnificent philosophy ... that will empirically and sensibly canvass the phenomena of nature'. Glanvill says that one of the more important ways of advancing knowledge is 'by enlarging the history of things', for such a natural history is 'fundamentally necessary to all the designs of science'. Sprat tells us that in pursuit of Bacon's aim of making 'faithful records, of all the works of nature or art, which can come within ... reach', the Royal Society sent out, world-wide, letters and questionnaires on all conceivable topics, discussing and debating the replies at their meetings.

The compilation of natural histories was only one part of Bacon's method. It was, similarly, only one strand in the ideas of many in the Royal Society. In general, however, it was not the second part of Bacon's Inductive Method that found favour. We have already seen that Hobbes and Gassendi diverged from Bacon's belief that the scrutiny of natural histories would enable one to reach certainty about the causes of things, and thought that one could produce conjectures and hypotheses at best. For Hobbes, such hypotheses were in terms of his 'indefinite' science based on the idea of matter in motion; for Gassendi, they were in terms of the Epicurean atomic or corpuscular theory which he adopted and developed. It was these ideas that found favour with the Royal Society. It was the belief of many of its members that if explanations and theories were to be given for the facts collected in their natural histories, they were to be given in mechanical terms, specifically in terms of the corpuscular theory. This comes out notably in the case of Robert Boyle, for he, more than most, defended, explained, and provided experimental illustrations for the corpuscular hypothesis. His *Origin of Forms and Qualities according to the Corpuscular Philosophy* (1666) is a masterpiece of criticism of the Aristotelians' substantial forms, a detailed classic exposition of the corpuscular theory he wishes to put in their place, and, finally, a compendium of experiments and results, all explained and analysed in corpuscularian terms.

The works of the 'new philosophers' of the seventeenth century give the impression of confident invulnerability. Particularly in their polemical passages they have a freshness and directness, such assurance that the world is now *their* oyster, that it is easy to forget that they did not go uncriticized. But criticisms there were. For example, Méric Casaubon, a prolific classical scholar, made out a good case for supposing there to be much of human value in the tradition he wished to defend. He objected to the stress the virtuosi laid on observation and experiment, on the grounds that it was likely to lead to atheism. 'Men that are much fixed upon matter ... may ... forget that there be such things in the world as Spirits ... and at last that there is a God, and that their souls are immortal.' He advocated 'Notional' studies which, having 'nothing to do with the senses', are 'therefore more divine'. He suggested, also, that an undue concentration on the new natural philosophy might lead to a certain intellectual arrogance. 'May not a man go too far in this study, and overvalue his progress so far, as to think nothing out of his reach?' So far as Gassendi and (as we shall see) Locke were concerned this objection is misplaced for, having a modest and moral view of our proper concerns, they retain an element of scepticism about man's ability to know. But Casaubon is not without insight in his idea that the committed experimental philosopher may come to think that all areas of human concern and experience are legitimate grist to his mill. In illustration of the absurdity of this 'scientific' arrogance, and teaching a lesson which is just as applicable today, he appeals to a story Gassendi told about a friend who watched a fight between a louse and a flea through a microscope. The man claimed to have learnt self-control, temperance, and forbearance from his observations, and to have 'profited more to rule his passions in the rest of his life, than he had done by any thing that he had heard, or read before'. Casaubon ridicules the idea that the straightforward collection of factual data about fleas and lice can provide the moral and civilizing education of the sort given by a study of the wise and sensitive works of humane literature. He sarcastically suggests that the story was probably invented 'to gratify some friends, who would be glad to hear what use can be made, even in point of life and manners, of a microscope'.

Casaubon was not alone in his criticisms of the new experimental philosophy for its atheistical tendencies. The claim that its concentration on things material meant a neglect, or even a denial, of things spiritual, a forgetfulness of God, was a common one. According to Richard Baxter, for example, it led to the arrogance of 'idle boys who tear out all the hard leaves of their books and say they have learned all when they have learned the rest'. The new philosophers 'cut off and deny the noblest parts of nature and then sweep together the dust of agitated atoms and tell us that they have resolved all the phenomena in nature'. It was, moreover, an accusation to which its adherents in the Royal Society were extremely sensitive. Though Hobbes had already made enemies of John Wallis and Seth Ward, two of its founder members, over his claim to have solved the geometrical problem of squaring the circle, it was at least partly due to his association in the popular mind with a materialistic atheism that he never became a Fellow. Indeed, 'the weightiest, and most solemn part' of Sprat's *History* is 'to make a defence of the Royal Society, and this new experimental learning, in respect of the Christian Faith'.

A common defence, and one for which Robert Boyle is prominent, was to develop the idea that, since the natural world is God's creation, the study of it leads towards, not away from, things spiritual. 'The knowledge of the works of God proportions our admiration of them, they participating and disclosing so much of the inexhausted perfections of their author, that the further we contemplate them, the more footsteps and impressions we discover of the perfections of their Creator.' It is interesting to note, moreover, that Locke, Boyle, and, particularly, Glanvill, all cite witchcraft as an observable phenomenon which directly shows the existence of a spiritual realm.

Though their general concentration on observation of the material world was thought to encourage atheism, it was the new philosophers' revival of Epicurus' atomistic conception of the world which particularly aroused criticism. Despite the fact that Gassendi and Boyle took care to find a place for God and the soul in their revivals of the theory, its adherents had perpetually to struggle against the undeniable fact that Epicurus had introduced it as a foundation for his explicit materialistic atheism.

One early member of the Royal Society was John Locke, who was elected in 1668. Though Locke did go in for some experimental work, his main contribution to the ethos of the Society was to do what Bacon had quite failed to do. He provided a theoretical justification for the method of collecting natural histories. More generally, he gives a lengthy defence and articulation of the idea that knowledge is ultimately dependent on the senses. For this reason, Locke is often called the father of modern empiricism.

6

John Locke (1632–1704)

The son of a lawyer and stern Puritan Parliamentarian, John Locke was born in Somerset in 1632, and died in Essex in 1704. He was educated at Westminster School and Christ Church, Oxford, where he studied, and later taught, subjects such as logic, moral philosophy, rhetoric, and Greek. He was interested in medicine too, and it was as medical adviser that, in 1666, he entered the service of Lord Ashley, later the Lord Chancellor and Earl of Shaftesbury. These academic and scientific interests did not fully occupy him. He also became involved in Protestant politics as secretary to Shaftesbury who, in the early 1680s, took part in the attempt to exclude James, the Catholic Duke of York, from succeeding to the throne of his brother Charles II. From 1675 to 1679 Locke travelled and studied in France; and from 1683 to 1689 he was in exile in Holland, his political views and associations having made it necessary for him to flee England. He returned after the 'Glorious Revolution', which replaced James II by the Protestant William of Orange. He then began a period in which he combined private study and writing with public service as Commissioner of Appeals and of the Board of Trade and Plantations.

Locke wrote and published on a considerable variety of topics: not only on various branches of philosophy, but also on education, economics, theology, and medicine. He is famous mainly for *An Essay Concerning Human Understanding* (1690) and his *Two Treatises of Government* (1690). But his *Letters concerning Toleration* (1689–92), *Some Thoughts concerning Education* (1693), and *The Reasonableness of Christianity* (1695) are important too.

Though it did not appear until relatively late in his life, Locke had been working on the *Essay* since about 1660. As he explains in the 'Epistle to the Reader', he began it after a discussion in which it occurred to him and his friends that they might get further with the problems which concerned them if they were first to 'examine our own abilities, and see, what objects our understandings were, or were not fitted to deal with'. The eventual result of this examination was the *Essay*, whose explicit aim is to 'enquire into the origin, certainty, and extent of human knowledge; together, with the grounds and degrees of belief, opinion, and assent'. According to one of its members, James Tyrrell, the group had been concerned with the 'principles of morality and revealed religion'. Presumably they were asking how the principles of morality are discovered and known to be true, and discussing the role of revelation as a source and foundation of morality and religion. This would certainly explain how they came to feel the need to have some wider understanding of how, and to what extent, we can acquire knowledge of any sort.

Locke's particular interest in religious and moral knowledge, and his more general interest in knowledge as such, falls in with the widespread concern with such matters which was consequent on the sixteenth-century rediscovery of ancient Greek scepticism. He speaks of a kind of intellectual pessimism, a 'despair of knowing anything', into which it is possible to fall after repeated failures in the search for knowledge. Men often 'raise questions, and multiply disputes, which never coming to any clear resolution, are proper only to continue and increase their doubts, and to confirm them at last in perfect scepticism'. Given the arguments of the sceptics, such failures are only to be expected of course; aiming to replace anxious intellectual despair with a calm peace of mind, the traditional Pyrrhonian response would have been to advocate suspension of judgement. Like Bacon and Hobbes, whose forthright reactions are that what is really needed is simply the adoption of a correct method, Locke does not immediately follow this traditional course; but he advances the more circumspect suggestion that we should first stand back and investigate our capacity for knowledge. We should see if there is a 'horizon ... between what is, and what is not comprehensible by us'. If we find that human faculties and understandings are such that knowledge is necessarily limited, we might more easily and 'with less scruple acquiesce in the avowed ignorance' of what lies beyond the horizon, and 'employ [our] ... thoughts and discourse, with more advantage and satisfaction' about what lies within our reach.

Some such open acceptance of our intellectual limitations would not be unrelated to Pyrrhonian *ataraxia* or peace of mind; but although Locke does, indeed, conclude that the truth often outruns our ability to know it, he certainly does not accept that *nothing* can be known. Although he does not adopt the frontal assault of Bacon on the 'perfect darkness' of a despairing scepticism, and eventually advocates a patient acceptance of our limitations, these limitations are, for him, not complete. He concludes that, although there are indeed some things we cannot and would be immodest to hope to know, there are others that we can know. Moreover, what we can know, such as our duties and obligations to each other and to God, is just what we need to know; and in many other cases we have beliefs sufficiently well-founded for the purposes of our everyday life. 'Men have reason to be well satisfied with what God hath thought fit for them, since he has given them ... whatsoever is necessary for the conveniences of life, and information of virtue.' Gassendi had suggested that it shows improper pride for a person who has feet to take him where he wants to go to 'yearn to fly like the birds'. Using this very image, Locke dwells on the thought at greater length, and provides a sharp contrast to the opinion of our own day, that unlimited scientific research is a valuable end in itself which needs no justification. He stresses that 'our business here is not to know all things, but those which concern our conduct'.

Against this background Locke begins his inquiry into the origin and extent of knowledge. Noting that we do have many ideas and beliefs, he asks what is perhaps the most basic question of epistemology: 'How comes ... [the mind] to be furnished? Whence comes it by that vast store of [ideas]? ... Whence has it all the materials of ... knowledge?' His answer is ringingly clear, and firmly places him as an empiricist. 'I answer, in one word, from *Experience*: in that, all our knowledge is founded; and from that it ultimately derives itself.' This answer is worked out in detail as the *Essay* proceeds, but it is important at the outset to see what it amounts to. We can do this by considering the reply

Locke makes, in an early draft of the *Essay*, to an objection which he might seem to invite.

The objection is that much of what we know could not have been learnt on the basis of experience. We know that all numbers are either even or odd, and that a whole is equal to the sum of its parts. But we surely do not know these on the basis of experience. As Henry Lee, one of Locke's critics, put it, such

general propositions ... [are] certainly true ... yet we can come to no knowledge of them *merely* by our senses; because *they* cannot reach to all the particulars included in the subjects of them. Our *senses* may inform us that any *single* whole is equal to *all* its parts; but not that all wholes in the world are so, unless we could suppose, that we had seen or felt them all.

For this reason, many in the seventeenth century would have said that such knowledge, together with knowledge of undoubted moral principles, such as that promises should be kept, is innate. It cannot be learnt from experience, and so must be something with which we are innately endowed.

Locke obviously recognized the implausibility of supposing that experience gives us these pieces of knowledge; experience cannot account for their certain applicability to *all* wholes, *all* numbers, or *all* promises. But his response is to reject the dichotomy which the objection presupposes: that such knowledge is either learnt from experience, or is innate. He reiterates that all knowledge is 'ultimately' derived from the senses, but explains that this does not mean that it directly comes from it. What experience initially and directly provides is not fully fledged knowledge itself, but 'the materials of knowledge', what he calls 'ideas'.

Our knowledge that all wholes are equal to the sum of their parts, or that any number is either even or odd, presupposes, or is expressed in terms of, the ideas of 'whole', 'part', 'number', 'evenness', and 'oddness'. It is these *ideas* that come from experience. Once we have them, our reason considers them and we come to see that wholes are equal to the sum of their parts, or that all numbers are even or odd. It is not part of Locke's empiricism that we know these things by observation and experience. What experience gives us is not knowledge itself, but the ideas which form the material basis for knowledge.

This means that Locke has not only to substantiate the claim
that all ideas are derived from experience, but also to explain how
it is that our reason gets from those ideas to certain items of
knowledge which others said were innate. Not everyone recognized this second requirement. Like Locke, Samuel Parker rejected innate knowledge. He objected (and Locke would have
agreed), that since truths such as that any number is even or odd
are quite obvious and self-evident, it would be pointless for God
to have imprinted them on our minds. But, unlike Locke, Parker
omitted to account for this self-evidence, and so laid himself open
to the objection of James Lowde, a defender of innateness, that
such truths would not have been self-evident were they not innate.
It is precisely because they are innate, Lowde said, that they are
obvious and self-evident to us. These truths 'owe their clearness
and evidence to their being thus imprinted. ... The needlessness
of imprinting such evident notions cannot be argued from their
present clearness; because it is their being thus imprinted or thus
connatural to our minds that makes them so.'

The bulk of Book 1 of the *Essay* consists of arguments against
innateness. It is often thought that these are supported by the
arguments in Book 2 for the view that all ideas, the materials of
knowledge, come from experience. But Locke's real target in
Book 1 is not innateness of ideas, but innateness of knowledge.
His arguments against innateness have their complement, not in
Book 2, but in Book 4, where he explains how we come to have
knowledge by reasoning about our ideas. It is true that sometimes
he does attack innate ideas; but this is merely an indirect strategy.
Since no knowledge could be innate unless its materials or constituent ideas were, any argument against innate ideas is, in effect,
an argument against innate knowledge.

The innately known truths which some people postulated were
not all of a piece. They were all 'obvious' truths; but some were
non-evaluative propositions, such as that wholes equal the sum
of their parts, while others were various principles of morality.
Locke's motives for rejecting them, accordingly, vary from case
to case. His worry about the 'practical' principles of morality is
that the doctrine of their innateness prevents people working them
out for themselves. Mistakenly supposing that their moral beliefs

are innately given, people are liable to continue to accept what they have been taught as young children. As for abstract 'speculative' principles, Locke's attacks on them stem partly from his dissatisfaction with scholasticism. 'Axioms' or 'maxims', such as that wholes equal the sum of their parts, were among the premisses of the demonstrative syllogisms of the doctrine of *scientia*, and some seventeenth-century developments of the doctrine said that they were innate. His motives aside, Locke's actual arguments against the doctrine of innate knowledge tend not to show it false, but only unnecessary, or lacking sound support. For one thing, all knowledge is explicable on the basis of the abilities we have to find it for ourselves. For another, there are, in fact, no propositions with a universal acceptance, and therefore none which need to be explained by supposing them to be innate. He does not, however, make the powerful point which had some currency at the time, that even were there universally accepted beliefs which were innate, this would not make them true, and so something we *knew*. Believing our intellectual abilities to be God-given, he presumably thought that, had they not been sufficient for our needs, God would not have supplemented them by innately endowing us with anything other than truth.

Locke's claim that prior to experience the mind is 'white paper, void of all characters', and that all its ideas, the materials of knowledge, come from that source, had been made earlier by Gassendi, but he defends and explains it at much greater length. 'Experience' is, in fact, a dual source of ideas. Some ideas come from 'sensation', from our sensory interaction with the world. 'Our senses ... do convey into the mind, several distinct perceptions of things ... and thus we come by those ideas we have of yellow, white, [etc.]' Others, such as the ideas of perceiving, willing, and doubting, come from 'reflection', from our 'perception of the operations of our own minds ... as it is employed about the ideas it has got [from sensation]'. But all the contents of our thought, however abstract and removed from experience they may be, have their source there.

All those sublime thoughts, which tower above the clouds, and reach as high as Heaven itself, take their rise and footing here: in all that great extent wherein the mind wanders, in those remote speculations it may seem to be elevated with, it stirs not one jot beyond those ideas, which *Sense* or *Reflection*, have offered.

Locke's contemporaries often criticized his continual talk of 'ideas', for which he apologized. 'Ideas' have played a part in philosophy at least as far back as Plato, for whom they had a reality of their own quite apart from any relation they might have to our minds. For Locke, however, they are 'whatsoever is the object of the understanding when a man thinks'; and his conception of them as essentially mind-dependent things is derived from Descartes. According to this conception, ideas may be internal sensations like pain; they may be perceptions of external objects and their qualities. They can be the medium of memory and imagination; they can figure in thinking, and in the understanding of language. Locke was not much interested in their exact nature: are they mental states or modifications, like waves in the sea, or mental entities in their own right, like flotsam on it? He thought that the answer to such questions was of little consequence for what he wanted to say.

It is plausible to say that our ideas of various colours, of various material things such as gold or sheep, or of processes and activities such as dancing and wrestling, derive from experience. But what of the ideas we have of a centaur, of God, of infinity, or of an as yet unbuilt house? We have had no experience of the objects of these ideas. Locke's distinction between *complex* ideas, and the *simple* ideas which are their component parts, copes with this. For simple ideas we are certainly directly beholden to experience. But though the parts of a complex idea must, in some way, have come from experience, the complexes themselves need not have, for we can construct them from their parts. This appeal to the idea of analysing complex mental thoughts into constituent simples was made earlier by Gassendi, and also carried on by philosophers in later centuries. Locke does not mean, though, that ideas are necessarily received *in their simplicity*: complexes can be got directly from experience, and do not always actually have to be built up from experienced simples. Indeed, he may not mean that they ever are received in their simplicity. Sometimes he implies that they can be, but at other times he speaks as though they are always 'observed to exist in several combinations'. In this latter case we get to simples by a process of 'Abstraction'. Locke aims to defend his view that all our ideas derive from experience by consideration of cases such as 'Space, Time, and Infinity, and some few others'. Besides being good test cases, Locke obviously finds these ideas intrinsically interesting too. One thing that appears in his discussion of them is a preparedness to say that a 'simple' idea may not be absolutely, and in all contexts, simple. Evidently he thinks of the distinction as being no more than a useful device for developing and explaining his claim, that all ideas derive from experience.

We have seen that Locke agrees that some things which we know, such as that all numbers are even or odd, could not be learnt directly from experience, and that he explains that he never meant otherwise, for what experience gives us is not knowledge itself, but its materials in the form of ideas. But we have also seen that he denies that such knowledge is innate and that its self-evidence arises from its being imprinted on our minds prior to all experience. What then *does* he think? How *does* knowledge arise?

Knowledge, Locke says, is 'the perception of the connection and agreement, or disagreement and repugnancy of any of our ideas'. Certain propositions are true because the relevant ideas are connected and related to each other in such a way as to make them true. Any number is even or odd by virtue of there being a connection between the idea of 'number' and those of 'evenness' or 'oddness'. It is by 'perceiving' these relations between ideas that we come to have knowledge. As Locke says, 'in some of our ideas there are certain relations, habitudes and connections, so visibly included in the nature of the ideas themselves, that we cannot conceive them separable from them, by any power whatsoever'. Many of us know that the three angles of a triangle add up to two right angles, and we know it because we 'perceive that equality to two right ones, does necessarily agree to, and is inseparable from the three angles of a triangle'. Sometimes the perception of connection between two ideas is direct, we perceive it 'immediately ... without the intervention of any other'. This gives us 'intuitive' knowledge, as when we see immediately that two and one are three. At other times a connection can be perceived only indirectly via the medium of other connections and ideas. Our knowledge of the angles of a triangle is of this 'demonstrative' sort, since here one has to 'find out some other angles, to which the three angles of a triangle have an equality; and finding those equal to two right ones, [one] comes to know their equality to two right ones'. Where either intellectual incapacity or lack of any actual connection means that we can neither intuitively nor demonstratively perceive a connection, then, 'though we may fancy, guess, or believe, yet we always come short of knowledge'.

This account of knowledge seems to disqualify much that we might ordinarily count as such. It is plausible to see our geometrical knowledge as based on 'perception' of connections between various ideas. But what of the knowledge that iron rusts when left out in the rain? What of the knowledge that gold is malleable, and pencil lead not? This surely is based on observation, experience, and informal experiment, not on intellectual perception of any connection between ideas. Doesn't Locke's definition rule it out from being knowledge at all? Indeed it does, and Locke recognizes such cases where, because there is 'a want of *a discoverable connection* between those ideas which we have . . . we are . . . left only to observation and experiment'. He explicitly says they do not constitute 'knowledge' but what he calls 'belief' or 'opinion'.

'Demonstrative' and 'intuitive' knowledge, acquired by perceiving connections between ideas, is 'certain and universal'. When we rationally see a connection between being a triangle, and having angles equal to two right angles, we see that *all* triangles *must* have angles like that. We cannot 'conceive . . . [the connection] separable from the ideas'. On the other hand, when we can intellectually see no connection between, for example, being gold and being malleable (when we have learnt of this property of gold only from experience), we do not know that gold *must* be malleable. We may 'believe', or be of the 'opinion', that it is universally and certainly true that it is; but, in relying on experience and observation, we do not 'know'.

Locke's distinction between 'knowledge' and 'belief' or 'opinion' has, in effect, been acknowledged by later philosophers. Though they more usually refer to a later distinction of Hume's, between 'relations of ideas' and 'matters of fact', recent philosophers have commonly distinguished cases where we proceed, in Locke's words, by 'the contemplation of our own abstract ideas' from those where, because there is no 'discoverable connection' between our ideas, we have to fall back on observation and experiment. They have tended, however, to treat this as a distinction between *two sorts of knowledge*, rather than between knowledge and something else. What Locke calls 'knowledge' they have called 'a priori knowledge'; what he calls 'opinion' or 'belief' they have called 'a posteriori' or 'empirical knowledge'. Locke's distinction can be related to earlier ones too. It echoes Gassendi's distinction between knowledge of natures and necessary causes, on the one hand, and the experience- and observation-based knowledge of appearances, on the other; it echoes Hobbes's between philosophical knowledge or knowledge based on 'true ratiocination', and what he calls 'experience'. At various points it is also related to the scholastic distinction between knowledge and opinion. This last comparison is worth elaborating.

Just as, for the Aristotelians, knowledge or *scientia* has to do with necessities, with what must be so and cannot be otherwise, so, for Locke, 'knowledge' is universal and certain. This is not to say that Locke accepts all the details of the scholastic account of *scientia* any more than Gassendi did. He does not think that knowledge is acquired by demonstrative syllogisms which have maxims and definitions for premisses; in many places in the *Essay* he criticizes various parts of this view.

The relationship between the Aristotelians and Locke on 'opinion' is less straightforward. Unlike *scientia*, the pursuit of which was the proper use of man's reason, mere opinion was traditionally supposed to be not worthy, or even capable, of systematic attention; the very word 'system' was out of place with it. Like Gassendi, however, Locke thinks 'opinion' worth having and searching after. Observation and experiment in order to discover the properties of things in the material world is a worthwhile activity; so much so that Locke sometimes honours its results with the more dignified term 'experimental knowledge'. In effect, he thinks that there can be a system or body of 'opinion'; this, after all, is what the new 'natural philosophy' is. But despite the transitional talk of 'experimental knowledge', Locke insists that 'natural philosophy is not capable of being made a science'. 'Natural philosophy' does not consist of 'knowledge', which arises from perception of connections between ideas, but of 'opinion'; and Locke still associates the word 'science' with *scientia* and 'knowledge' proper. To this extent, Locke agrees with the scholastic, Thomas Sergeant, that 'the way of experiments cannot be a true method to science'. But, even if not properly speaking a science, it is still worthy of systematic pursuit. The idea of a systematic and serious, observationally and experientially based study of nature, called 'natural philosophy', was one which Locke shared with others of course, and in particular with his colleagues in the Royal Society. It goes along with the common complaint that there are areas and methods of serious investigation which are just not touched by scholastic doctrines.

A further complexity in the comparison between Locke and the Aristotelians is that their 'opinion' concerns contingencies, things which are so, but which might have been otherwise. At first sight this may seem so for Locke too. He denies that we *know* that gold is malleable, because for us there is no 'universal certainty' about it. Unless we make it trivially true that gold is malleable, by explicitly including malleability in our idea of it, we can perceive no connection between the ideas of gold and malleability; our observation and experiment do not tell us that gold *must* be malleable; we have no *knowledge* that it is. But the fact that *we* can perceive no connection does not, for Locke, mean that there may not be one there. So, while for the scholastic tradition 'opinion' concerns contingencies, for Locke it concerns what *seem* like contingencies to us, but what, in reality, may be universal certainties. He explains this important possibility, of there being connections which we cannot perceive, in terms of features of various sorts of complex idea.

The distinctions between kinds of complex idea are considered at some length in the *Essay*. Having divided ideas into simple and complex, he introduces three sorts of complex idea: 'modes', 'substances', and 'relations'. He does not say a lot about relations, and often treats them along with modes. They concern 'comparing' or 'referring' one thing with, or to, another. The property of being whiter is an obvious example, for one thing is compared with another when we say it is whiter than the other. They also concern the mind being 'led' from one thing 'to something beyond'. When Caius is mentioned as being a husband, our minds are led to a woman whose husband he is. Much more is said about 'substances' and 'modes', and the distinction between them is important in Locke's theory of knowledge. The ideas of 'triangle' and 'gratitude' are modes, those of 'gold' and of 'man' are substances. Their 'complexity' is relatively straightforward. The idea of a triangle is made up from the ideas of being a closed figure, and having three straight sides; the idea of gold from those of yellowness, malleability, and fusibility. But why is one a 'mode', and the other a 'substance'?

'Substances' are ideas of 'things subsisting by themselves'. It is plain from Locke's examples that they (or, strictly, the things of which they are ideas) are naturally occurring kinds of material thing or stuff. They are, in fact, just the kind of thing the natural philosopher might be interested in. Like both the Aristotelians and Gassendi, Locke talks of their 'natures' or 'essences', but in doing so he makes a sharp distinction between 'real' and 'nominal' essence. The scholastics would have recognized some such distinction. Besides a 'real' definition which exhibits the 'form' or 'essence' of what a thing really is, a form which explains the possession by a thing of its characteristic properties, they allowed for a 'nominal' definition which captures only those properties themselves. But, like Gassendi, Locke rejects 'forms'. For him, definitions are not 'real', they do not define things; they are nominal and define words. The definition of gold is simply what *we* mean by the word, the complex idea or nominal essence *we* have in our minds when we speak of it. This idea or *nominal essence* will vary from person to person; goldsmiths know more properties of gold, and so have a different idea of it than does a child.

What, then, of Locke's 'real essence'? Following Gassendi and Boyle, he rejects the forms of the scholastics as explanations of why material things have the properties they do, and substitutes instead an adapted Epicurean atomism as the basis for explanation. Accordingly, for him, the real essence of gold, which accounts for and explains those properties of gold with which we are familiar, and which constitute our idea or nominal essence of it, is its corpuscular or atomic constitution.

Locke's distinction between the real and nominal essence of substances, and the way in which the corpuscular hypothesis figures in his conception of the world, which he shares with other anti-scholastics of the time, is brought out nicely by his analogy of the Strasburg Cathedral clock. Locke's contemporaries marvelled at this human creation just as they marvelled at nature as seen through the microscope. The clock did a lot more besides telling the time of day. For example, it incorporated a globe of the heavens with a revolving sun and moon, an astrolabe showing the positions of the planets, statues which sounded bells, and a mechanical cock. Gassendi spoke of our not knowing the corpuscular nature of things, the 'inner shrines' of nature, but only their appearances; similarly, the 'gazing countryman', as Locke calls him, would know only the clock's outer show, and not its internal mechanism. The 'nominal essence' of the clock is the idea we have of it, and as with gold, this will vary from person to person. One observer may have been particularly impressed by the figure of Death sounding the hours on a bell, and his idea will include that. Another, who did not pass by on the hour, might think, not of Death, but of the astrolabe showing the positions of the planets. Though different in detail, these ideas are similar, in that they both derive from the clock's observable characteristics and behaviour. For Conrad Dasypodius, however, the mathematician at Strasburg Academy who designed and planned the clock, the nominal essence would be radically different. He would understand in detail the working of the mechanism of the clock, which enables it to function as it does. His general idea, his 'nominal essence', of the clock would be an idea of what is, in effect, its 'real essence'.

This work of art provided an analogy for works of nature such as gold. They both have observable features and properties. The clock has moving hands and figures; gold is yellow, malleable, soluble in some acids, and not in others. Then, just as the clock, and clocks like it, have a certain inner mechanical constitution from which these features arise, so has gold in the view of those who adopted the corpuscular hypothesis. The different performances of other clocks correspond to different mechanisms; the differences in quality of different substances, the yellowness of gold, or the silvery colour of lead, similarly correspond to differences in the shape, size, arrangement, and state of motion of their corpuscles.

But there is an important difference between the clock, which is what Locke calls an 'artificial substance', and naturally occurring substances such as gold. The clock's designer would know the details of its real essence whereas, says Locke, none of us know the real essence of gold. Our sensory capacities are too limited. Beyond conceiving it in corpuscular terms, we have no idea of it. For the horologist the nominal essence of the clock *is* an idea of its real essence; in this he differs from the gazing countryman, to whom the nominal essence is simply some combination of various observable features. But so far as natural substances go we are all gazing countrymen. The nominal essence of gold, our idea of it, is not an idea of its real essence.

Properties of the kind which go to make up our nominal essence of gold are divided by Locke into 'primary and original' and 'secondary' (and also 'tertiary'). This famous and much-discussed distinction between primary and secondary qualities has historical antecedents in Galileo, Descartes, and Hobbes. Since it was generally associated with the corpuscular theory of matter it was a common idea in Locke's time, though its details, and the arguments from which it was derived, were not always the same. Primary qualities belong not only to observable substances such as gold, but also to the minute corpuscles which make them up. A piece of gold has solidity, extension, shape, 'mobility' (is in motion or at rest), and 'number' (is one piece), and according to the corpuscular theory the gold's corpuscles have these qualities too. Secondary (and tertiary) qualities, such as colour and taste (and solubility in certain acids), belong to a piece of gold but not to its corpuscles.

According to the corpuscular theory these secondary (and tertiary) qualities arise from the arrangement, the 'texture', of the solid, shaped, and mobile corpuscles which constitute gold, and so are not to be attributed to the corpuscles themselves. Of course, like its colour, gold's primary qualities of solidity and extension also result from its consisting of solid, extended corpuscles. What distinguishes them from secondary (and tertiary) qualities is that they are those features which corpuscles need to have in order to account for *all* the qualities (primary, secondary, and tertiary) of the substances which they make up.

Because observable substances consist of arrangements of insensible corpuscles, they are able to act on each other and on our sense-organs in certain ways. Interaction between the corpuscles of gold and those of sulphuric acid results in these arrangements being changed, a change we describe as the solution of gold in the acid. Interaction between the corpuscles of an almond and those of our taste-buds results in the production, in our minds, of a certain idea, that of sweetness; though quite how such causation between the physical and the mental takes place is, Locke says, a mystery which we do not understand. Similarly, via the intermediary of reflected light rays, interaction between the corpuscles of gold and those of our eyes produces in us the idea of yellowness. Secondary qualities of objects are those arrangements of its corpuscles which cause certain ideas *in us* as sentient beings. Tertiary qualities are those arrangements which change, or can be changed by, the corpuscular arrangements *of other things*.

Fire causes the idea of pain in us, and snow causes ideas of coldness and of whiteness. However, while we think of pain simply as an idea caused in us by interaction between the fire and our bodies, we think of the snow as being, in itself, white and cold. Locke suggests that his corpuscular account of objects, and our perception of them, gives us no reason to think of snow's coldness and whiteness like this. We do perceive snow as being cold and white in itself; but since our doing so is a result of the *texture* of primary qualitied corpuscles, there is no need to suppose snow really is as we percieve it. Snow does have a certain corpuscular arrangement, which fits it to produce ideas of coldness and of whiteness in us; but just as there is nothing in fire resembling our idea of pain, so there need be nothing in snow resembling the whiteness and coldness it appears to have. The case is otherwise with respect to primary qualities. In order to explain how we perceive objects as having shape, and being solid, we need to suppose objects have those properties in the way they appear to have.

Besides defining substances as complex ideas of 'distinct particular things subsisting by themselves', Locke also says that the main component of such a complex is 'the supposed, or confused idea of Substance', something he also calls 'substratum' or 'pure substance in general'. Locke's references to 'Substance' or 'substratum' have become notorious, and there are different accounts of what he means by them. Often they are taken as implying a rejection of the kind of view which was held by Bertrand Russell and, less recently, by Isaac Watts. According to this view the grammatical difference between nouns and adjectives marks no real difference between things and their properties: a material thing, a substance, is no more than 'a bundle' of properties. As opposed to this, Locke is often supposed to be saying that, in addition to properties, things have a 'substratum' which 'supports' their properties. According to a second account, Locke's 'substratum' should not be related to such abstract logical questions about the difference between 'things' and 'properties'. It should be identified either in a general way with matter as understood by the corpuscularians or, more specifically, with the particular arrangements or 'textures' of corpuscles which constitute real essences.

There is a further topic in connection with Locke's complex ideas of substances which needs some discussion. There are various particular material substances such as gold and lead, of which we have various ideas. What do they have in common that makes them material substances? What, in other words, is our 'idea of Body' as such? In Locke's view, it is an idea of 'an extended solid substance, capable of communicating motion by impulse'. His belief that solidity is an essential part of body was shared with others, such as Boyle and Newton. According to the rival belief of the Cartesians, however, body was constituted by extension alone, and not also by either solidity or the ability to communicate motion. Descartes says that 'the nature of matter or of body ... does not consist in its being hard, or heavy, or coloured ... but solely in the fact that it is a substance extended in length, breadth, and depth.'

Locke rejects this, though his arguments against Descartes's identification of body with extension tend to be little more than initial difficulties. He objects that extension, by itself, is insufficient to constitute body; this property of filling space, like the ability to communicate motion in collisions, must depend *on something else*. This, he says, is solidity or 'impenetrability'. Furthermore, 'body' is so plainly different from 'space' that extension cannot be its *whole* essence. Body can be divided into parts which can be moved away from each other; space cannot. Body is not, or is not necessarily, unlimited; space is. If body and space were identical there would be no empty space, and motion would be impossible. But Descartes had already given answers to objections such as these. The difference between space and body is only 'in our mode of conceiving it'. Motion *is* possible even without empty space; so long as things simultaneously move into each other's places, motion is as possible in a plenum as in a crowd.

Although Descartes advocated a broadly 'mechanical philosophy', according to which the material world was to be understood in terms of matter and motion, he was not a standard corpuscularian or atomist. It follows from his identification of body and extension that there can be no empty space or vacuum, no Epicurean 'void' in which the atoms move. Cartesian matter is continuous, and there are no discrete atoms. The world is ultimately to be understood in terms of swirlings or 'vortices', in a matter which is identical with extension or space, not in terms of collisions of solid, impenetrable atoms moving in an otherwise empty space.

The more usual and non-Cartesian belief, that matter consists of discrete solid particles, raises the question of how these cohere together into the larger extended bodies of our ordinary experience. Locke asks how the 'solid parts of body ... [keep] united, or cohere together to make extension'. Given his scepticism about our ability to penetrate to the real essences of things, it is not surprising that he finds that none of the much-discussed contemporary theories on offer provide a satisfactory answer, and concludes that we are simply ignorant about this.

The extension of body, which for Descartes is its whole essence, is not for Locke the only consequence of what he sees as its essential property of solidity. The third part of the idea he says we have of body, its ability to communicate motion by impulse, follows from solidity too. We have, however, no more real understanding of this ability than we do of cohesion.

The two important kinds of complex idea which Locke distinguishes are 'substances' and 'modes'. The former, as we have been seeing, are ideas of material things, such as sheep, or of kinds of material stuff, such as gold. Their characteristic properties, many of which are included in our complex idea or nominal essence, are what the natural philosopher might collect, observe, and list in a 'natural history'. They result from their real essences, the arrangement of corpuscles which make them up. What, then, are 'modes'?

As Locke defines them, they 'contain not in them the supposition of subsisting by themselves, but are considered as dependences on, or affections of substances'. Given this and various of his examples, such as 'triangle' or 'procession', they seem to be ways in which the substances on which they depend may be ordered, organized, or arranged. A triangle is not a material thing, but a shape which material things may have, an arrangement into which they can be put. A procession is not a material thing, but a certain organization of material things. Locke describes modes as combinations of 'scattered and independent ideas' which are 'put together by the mind'. He describes them as 'creatures of the understanding', unlike substances which are 'works of nature'. This does not mean that they cannot be found in the world; a child may wonder what shape or arrangement a triangle is, and have it pointed out to him. It seems to mean that, whereas we form ideas of substances by observation of commonly conjoined properties and qualities, the modes we form depend on human conventions, purposes, and institutions. People form collections of ideas into modes, 'as they have frequent use of in their way of living and conversation, leaving others, which they have but seldom an occasion to mention, loose and without names.' We have no name for the killing of an older man, but do have a name for the killing of one's father.

Our ideas of substances, their nominal essences, are not ideas of their real essences. Our idea of gold is simply an idea of some of its observable properties, which are supposed to flow from its real essence. Our nominal essences of modes, however, *are* ideas of their real essences. With many of Locke's examples of modes it is not easy to see how this can be. Since it is not easy to see a distinction between their characteristic properties and some essence from which they flow, one might be tempted to think that, when Locke speaks of a coincidence of their real and nominal essence, he means that the notion of a real essence does not really apply to modes. But when he says that the real and nominal essences of a mode, such as a triangle, coincide, he really does mean what we should expect him to mean: that our idea of a triangle is like the horologist's idea of the Strasburg clock, an idea of its real essence, and not like that of the gazing countryman, an idea of some of its properties.

The real essences of modes are not corpuscular, of course. Triangles are not material things, but shapes which material things can have. But this does not mean that they have no essence from which their characteristic properties arise. Locke says that

figure including a space between three lines, is the real as well as nominal essence of a triangle; it being not only the abstract idea to which the general name is annexed, but the very *essentia*, or being, of the thing itself, that foundation from which all its properties flow, and to which they are all inseparably annexed. But it is far otherwise concerning that parcel of matter, which makes the ring on my finger, wherein these two essences are ... different.

Here Locke draws a parallel between modes such as triangles, and substances such as gold and the Strasburg clock. Gold has various properties as a result of its insensible corpuscular constitution; the clock has certain characteristic features as a consequence of its internal mechanism. Similarly, a figure of three lines enclosing a space, which is the idea we have of a triangle, has various properties as a consequence of being constructed in that way, properties such as having internal angles equal to two right angles, and external angles equal to internal opposites.

Locke's thought is that, just as we can distinguish between the characteristics of gold (or the clock), and its corpuscular constitution (or internal mechanism), so we can distinguish between the characteristic properties of a triangle, and what accounts for or explains them. We might think of the real essence of a triangle, 'three lines enclosing a space', as instructions for making such a figure: it is how that figure is constituted. When a figure is drawn according to these instructions it will, as a consequence, have various properties which a geometer might have predicted. Similarly, to take another case, we might think of the real essence of a circle, a figure which bears a constant relation to some one point, as an indication of how, along Hobbesian lines, to generate or construct one. It is as a result of being so constructed, and of being the figure it is, that a circle has its characteristic properties.

Given that 'knowledge' is the perception of connections between ideas, and that where this perception is lacking we have only 'belief' or 'opinion', it is Locke's view that geometry, unlike natural philosophy, constitutes a 'science', a body of 'knowledge'. It is also his view that our abstract ideas of modes, such as triangles and other geometrical figures, are ideas of their real essences, unlike those of substances, such as gold, which are merely ideas of observable properties which arise from their real essences. These two views go together. If our idea of gold were of its real essence,

then the properties we discover in that body, would depend on that complex idea, and be deducible from it, and their necessary connection with it be known; as all properties of a triangle depend on, and as far as they are discoverable, are deducible from the complex idea of three lines, including a space.

It is because we know the real essences of geometrical figures that that subject consists of 'certain and universal knowledge' obtained by a priori intuition or demonstration. But we do not know the real essences of the substances of natural philosophy, so all that we can do is to observe and list their properties, and form only beliefs and opinions about them.

Substances afford matter of very little general knowledge; and the bare contemplation of their abstract ideas, will carry us but a very little way in the search of truth and certainty. ... The want of ideas of their real essences sends us from our own thoughts, to the things themselves.

Since Hume, philosophers of an empiricist turn of mind have tended to suppose that any 'knowledge' obtained by a priori perception of connections between ideas is trifling and empty of content, and that the price paid for the necessity and certainty of such 'knowledge' is a loss of information. In this respect Locke is not an empiricist: he does not think that geometrical knowledge or, for that matter, the knowledge we would have in natural philosophy if we knew the real essences of substances, is empty and trivial. Having external angles equal to internal opposites *follows* from being a figure of three lines, but is no more a *part* of that idea than being yellow or malleable would be part of a detailed idea of the corpuscular constitution of gold.

In not finding a priori knowledge trivial, Locke does not fit our modern textbook descriptions of 'an empiricist'. He further fails to fit them in his belief that natural philosophy fails to be a science simply because we are ignorant of the relevant real essences, not because there are no necessary connections in nature. Modelled as it is on the a priori science of geometry, his ideal of a scientific natural philosophy is that of a textbook rationalist. It is unattainable, not because of the nature of things, but because of the nature of our faculties.

All of this forms a central part of Locke's answer to his initial question about the extent of human knowledge, and whether there is a horizon between what we can and cannot know. Our knowledge is bounded by our ideas, and extends only so far as they are ideas of real essences. But geometrical figures are not the only modes, and so are not the only things whose real essences we can know. The ideas of morality are modes too, and Locke thinks that with proper application we could develop a systematic science of ethics similar to that of mathematics and geometry. This possibility of a demonstrative science of ethics caught the imagination of Locke's friend William Molyneux, who pressed him to produce it. Locke replied that *he* could not do it; it would take someone of the intellectual stature of Newton. He believed, moreover, that although man's reason had gone some way in 'its great and proper business of morality', the progress had been slow. Yet, even though moral rules and principles are neither innate, nor easy to acquire by reason, no one need remain ignorant of his duties and obligations: the Bible gives us them. 'The Gospel', Locke explained to Molyneux, 'contains so perfect a body of ethics, that reason may be excused from that enquiry.' But taking our morality from the Bible does not necessarily mean merely taking it on trust and authority, and abandoning all thought of moral *knowledge*. Though our reason may fail us in *discovering* moral truths, it need not in *verifying* what the Bible says. We can find justifying arguments for its ethical contents, even if we could not come to them on our own. So long as, in the end, our grasp of them rests upon reason, we have knowledge, no matter how it was first suggested. But even though justification by hindsight is easier than discovery, some people are still not rationally able to see the truth of the Gospels for themselves; even though the Bible does point the way to moral knowledge, most people 'cannot know, and therefore they must believe'.

Where 'belief' is based not on experience and observation, but on the revelation of the Gospels, Locke speaks of 'faith'. Here he directly develops the interest which he and his friends in the discussion group had, and which had led to his starting work on the *Essay*: the relation and interplay between knowledge and reason on the one hand, and faith, belief, and revelation on the other. His general theme is that reason has supremacy over revelation. In that it gives us 'knowledge', as opposed to mere 'belief' or 'faith', of course it has; but Locke also means that revelation must be answerable to reason. If the Gospels gave a moral truth already known by reason, this would verify the Gospels, not our reason. Reason is more certain than revelation, and cannot be made any more certain by it. We need to be certain that the revelation stems from God; and we cannot be as certain of this as we are of our reason-based knowledge of the particular truth in question. This means that nothing *contrary* to reason can be accepted on the basis of supposed revelation. It would 'be to subvert the principles, and foundations of all knowledge ... if ... what we certainly know, give way to what we may possibly be mistaken in.'

Though moral truths do not, at least in principle, lie outside of reason, and beyond the horizon of our knowledge and under-standings, some things do. Though not 'contrary' to it, they are 'above reason'. We have already seen some such things in the area of natural philosophy, things of which, 'by the natural use of our faculties, we can have no knowledge at all'. Others have been the subject of revelation; for example, 'that the dead shall rise, and live again'. But, that revelation can tell us things 'above reason' does not make it superior to it. Reason cannot decide the truth or falsity of what is revealed in such cases, but can decide whether the revelation is genuine. A revelation from God is bound to be true, 'but whether it be a divine revelation, or no, *reason* must judge'.

Furthermore, our salvation does not depend on our putting 'faith' in anything 'above reason'. It is open to us simply by the use of our natural faculties. God has 'given all mankind so sufficient a light of reason, that they ... could not (whenever they set them-selves to search) either doubt of the being of a God, or of the obedience due to Him'. This idea that the essentials for salvation are never 'above reason' sits uneasily with what Locke has already said about the practical difficulty of working them out for oneself. A slow-minded or busy person can be thankful that the Bible 'contains so perfect a body of ethics that reason may be excused from the enquiry', but the position of those to whom it is un-available is not entirely happy.

Locke's belief in the relevance of reason to religion and moral-ity, and his claim that salvation can be won on its basis alone, were common from the time of the Restoration into the eighteenth century. The Civil War had seen an outburst of religious fanati-cism and the extremes of what was called 'enthusiasm'. With the Restoration there came a reaction against the supernatural and mysterious, against private 'revelations' and 'inspiration'. Mod-eration and reasonableness began to come to the fore. Thomas Sprat refers to 'the late extravagant excesses of enthusiasm. The infinite pretences to inspiration, and immediate communion with God.' He is clearly relieved that 'the fierceness of violent in-spirations is in good measure departed' and that 'the universal disposition of this age is bent upon a rational religion'.

For Locke, the regulation by reason of 'faith', or 'belief' based on revelation, distinguishes it from the 'ungrounded fancies', 'the conceits of a warmed and over-weening brain', which are characteristic of 'enthusiasm'. Divine inspiration and revelation are not their own guarantees, and we must always ask 'How do I know that God is the revealer of this to me?' Otherwise, 'how great soever the assurance is, that I am possessed with, it is groundless; whatever light I pretend to, it is but enthusiasm.'

The movements of Cambridge Platonism (involving Henry More, Benjamin Whichcote, and Ralph Cudworth), and of Latitudinarianism (involving many members of the Royal Society, such as Sprat and Glanvill) encouraged the idea that, by itself, reason could provide the essentials of religious belief and the means to salvation. At first, this stress on 'natural religion', as it was called, did not necessarily mean the abandonment of Christianity as revealed in the Scriptures; so long as it was not inconsistent with reason, it could be accepted. But towards the end of the century the ideal began to emerge that not merely the essentials, but also the whole of religion could be discovered by reason, and that nothing 'above reason' should be a part of it. Even though he did not actually advocate it, Locke certainly did much to foster such rational deism.

To inquire into 'the original, certainty, and extent' of human knowledge was the explicit aim of Locke's great masterpiece, the *Essay*. But in following him through that aim, we nevertheless have left untouched some of the ideas for which he is famous. Because of Berkeley's criticisms of them, Locke's views on language and abstract ideas, views which were implicit in the discussion of nominal essences, are best left for the next chapter. For the remainder of this one we will look at his account of personal identity and the mind, and then at his political philosophy.

Locke's discussion of personal identity, which was added in the second edition of the *Essay* on the suggestion of Molyneux, has been of lasting interest to philosophers. Early on he makes a general point, one taken up by later writers, that there is a relativity about identity. If we ask 'Is this what was here last year?' it matters what kind of thing *this* is. If we are referring to a mass of matter we can say that it is the same so long as it consists of the same particles, whereas if we are referring to a living body this need not be so: 'a colt grown up to a horse, sometimes fat, sometimes lean, is all the while the same horse: though ... there may be a manifest change of the parts.' In this second case, identity consists in matter being continuously arranged in a similar way so as to 'partake of the same life'. The point is important for, when he turns to personal identity, he insists on a distinction between two ideas which 'the ordinary way of speaking' runs together: the idea of 'man', and the idea of 'person'. The identity of a man is basically no different from that of any other animal. It consists in 'nothing but a participation of the same continued life, by constantly fleeting particles of matter, in succession vitally united to the same organized body'. The idea of a person, however, is not the idea of a living body of a certain kind. It is that of 'a thinking, intelligent being, that has reason and reflection, and can consider itself as itself, the same thinking thing in different times and places'. A person 'is self to itself now' and is always conscious of hs present thoughts, feelings, and actions; similarly, he 'will be the same self as far as the same consciousness can extend to actions past or to come'. Locke's description of a person as 'a thinking, intelligent being' does not mean that the continuity of self-consciousness which constitutes personal identity is the continuity of some immaterial substance, a soul, mind, or spirit, which is self-conscious, for he is clearly unhappy with a Cartesian view of ths sort.

Descartes distinguished two sorts of substance, souls (or minds or spirits), and matter (or body). Each has 'one principal property ... which constitutes its nature or essence'. In the case of body this, as we have already seen, is extension; in the case of mind it is thought. Persons, for Descartes, are mental or immaterial thinking substances. I am, says Descartes, 'a substance the whole essence or nature of which is to think. ... This "me", that is to say, the soul by which I am what I am, is entirely distinct from body ... and even if the body were not, the soul would not cease to be what it is.'

Just as he disagreed with him about the essential or principal properties of body, Locke disagreed with Descartes about the

mind. For one thing, besides 'thought', a further essential property in our idea of mind is the 'power of exciting motion in body,
by will, or thought'. Moreover, as Descartes means it, the view
that thought is essential to mind is the view that the mind 'always
thinks, and that it has the actual perception of ideas in itself
constantly, as long as it exists'. It is the view that actually occurring thought, rather than the mere ability or capacity to think, is
essential to mind. For Locke, however, actually being engaged in
thought is not essential to a mind or soul. For him, thinking is to
the soul as motion, not extension, is to the body. Just as a material
body may or may not actually be moving, so a mind may or may
not actually be thinking. By 'thought' Descartes did not just mean
deliberation, or some strictly intellectual activity; he took it to
include other forms of consciousness, such as imagining and feeling. But Locke's disagreement with him does not stem from this.
However widely one takes 'thought', it is neither self-evident nor
a fact of experience that we are always actually thinking. As Locke
says, 'every drowsy nod shakes their [the Cartesians'] doctrine.'

Besides disagreeing with Descartes about the exact constitution
of our *idea* of mind, Locke also disagreed with the claim that we
know the real nature of mind. Specifically, we do not know that
minds are immaterial substances whose nature does not go
beyond those properties we think are essential to them. The power
to move a body, and the ability to think, do constitute our idea
of mind. But we neither understand this power nor know, as
Gassendi had already argued against Descartes, 'wherein thinking
consists'. We do not know, for instance, whether thought might
not have a purely material basis, instead of being the unexplained
property of an immaterial substance.

It follows from Descartes's view of mind that personal identity
consists in the continuation of an immaterial substance, a mind
or soul. According to Locke, however, the question is 'what makes
the same *person*, and not whether it be the same identical substance, which always thinks in the same person, which in this case
matters not at all'. The identity of a horse can be preserved
through changes of matter; it does not depend on the identity of
a continued material substance, but on 'the unity of one continued
life'. Similarly, the identity of a person does not depend on the

continuity of an immaterial substance, a mind or soul. 'It being the same consciousness that makes a man be himself to himself, personal identity depends on that only, whether it be annexed only to one individual substance, or can be continued in a succession of several substances.'

The Cartesians concede something like this in the case of brute animal life. Not wanting to say that it has an immaterial soul, they allow that a horse has a continued identity despite changes of matter. So, since they claim to know the complete and final story about the nature of mental substance, it is incumbent on them to show that it is impossible for the same consciousness to be transferred from one substance to another. In truth, however, we just do not know whether this *is* impossible. Perhaps it is, perhaps it is not; our ignorance shows that what we mean when we speak of personal identity is continuity of consciousness, not of substance. Moreover, for all we know about the nature of thought, it might be possible, it might even be necessary, that the substances whose succession could continue a personal consciousness are material, not immaterial at all.

Even supposing that consciousness need not, or even cannot, have its basis in material substance, it is possible not only that the same personal consciousness be associated with different immaterial Cartesian substances, but also that the same immaterial substance be associated, at different times, with different consciousnesses. The analogy between the identity of a living body and that of personal identity makes this plausible. Not only might one living body consist of different particles of matter, but also different bodies (mine and the sheep that I eat, for example), might consist of the same matter.

For Locke, then, personal identity consists in an identity of consciousness, and not in the identity of some substance whose essence it is to be conscious. He agrees with the 'more probable opinion ... [that] this consciousness is annexed to, and the affection of one identical immaterial substance', but, expressing his general scepticism about the extent of our knowledge, he says we really do not know the truth of the matter.

Locke aroused considerable controversy with his suggestion that 'since we know not wherein thinking consists', it may be, for all we know, that nothing more than matter is necessary for thought, and that God might have 'given to some systems of matter fitly disposed, a power to perceive and think'. For one thing, it would have seemed to count against the idea of immortality, for it was commonly argued that only something immaterial could be immortal. Locke's view is, however, that '[all] the great ends of morality and religion, are well enough secured, without philosophical proofs of the soul's immateriality'. *If* God can make matter think in this world, and give us material 'souls', he can do so in the next. Whether we are purely material or not we cannot know; but being so would not be inconsistent with immortality, and we have the guarantee of revelation that we are, in fact, immortal. Locke's tentative suggestion about the possibility of thinking matter would have seemed to lead to atheism too; but he was quick to point out to his critic, Edward Stillingfleet, that the suggestion that *we* might be purely material does not involve the denial of all spiritual immaterial beings; if we *are* thinking matter, it needed a spiritual God to make us so.

Even apart from these wider consequences of his thought about persons, Locke's idea that their identity consists in continuity of self-consciousness came under attack. Thomas Sergeant, Joseph Butler, and Thomas Reid reasserted a continuous mental substance as the basis of personal identity, and said that the Lockean continuity of self-consciousness made no sense without it. Reid developed a rather more interesting objection, one made earlier by Berkeley, which puts the case of a general who is conscious of things he did as an officer, but no longer conscious, as he was when an officer, of what he did as a boy. For Locke, it was argued, the absurdity would follow that while the general is the same person as the officer, and he the same as the boy, the general is not the same person as the boy. Something of what Locke would have said to this is already contained in the *Essay*. It appears that, despite the way he first introduces the topic of personal identity, his detailed interest is not so much in what makes a person the same over time, but in the sense one has of oneself, one's past deeds and actions, and the relation of this to questions of moral praise and blame. In a famous sentence he says that '*Person* ... is a forensic term appropriating actions and their merit; and so belongs only to intelligent agents capable of a law, and happiness and misery.' At one point he talks of the extension over time of 'a personality' rather than of 'a person', and might have said that, even if the general knew what he did as a boy, it could be nothing to him, no part of his adult conception of himself, and so not a matter for guilt or blame. We do not, Locke points out, punish a person for what he did when temporarily insane, and we speak of him as having been 'not himself' or 'beside himself'. He allows that, despite his claiming to have no consciousness of them, a court may punish a man for his drunken actions, but this is only because it cannot be sure of distinguishing in the defendant's plea 'what is real, what counterfeit'. We may be assured that, on the Judgement Day, 'no one shall be made to answer for what he knows nothing of '. What is important is what a person is 'concerned and accountable' for, what he 'owns and imputes to ... *self* ', what his 'conscience [is] accusing or excusing him' of.

Reid's objection, which has been reiterated over the years, is often supplemented with its converse. Is it not possible for a person to 'remember' something he never did? Indeed, does not Locke himself raise this objection when he asks why 'one intellectual substance may not have represented to it, as done by itself, what it never did, and was perhaps done by some other agent'? The extent to which this is an objection to Locke's actual views will depend, as in the case of the brave officer, on whether they concern what makes a person at one time the same as he is at another, or concern moral matters of praise and blame. What is clear is that, in the above passage, he is not making the objection against himself. The possibility raised there is intended for the Cartesians to deal with. It is their view, and not any of his, that makes personal identity consist in the identity of the same thinking substance.

Locke's political philosophy is mainly contained in his anonymously published *Treatises of Government* (1690). He says in the preface that his hope is, 'to establish the throne of our great restorer, our present King William; to make good his title, in the consent of the people'. William had come to the throne two years earlier, in 1688, after the Glorious Revolution against the Catholic

James II; but although the *Treatises* do contain material which could be seen as after-the-fact justifications of the Revolution, they were not written for this reason. Having been started some ten years earlier, they were substantially complete by the early 1680s. They were composed in the years of the Exclusion crisis, during which Locke's patron, Shaftesbury, and others, sought to exclude James, then Duke of York, from the succession to the throne, and argued for government by consent and for the right to religious dissent. The *Treatises* supported such arguments, and it was his having, and being suspected by the government of having, such seditious views that made it necessary for Locke to flee to Holland in 1683.

The *First Treatise* is now less studied than the *Second*, for it is of less lasting philosophical importance. It consists mainly of criticism of the theories of absolute monarchy and the divine right of Kings, for which Robert Filmer had argued in his post-humously published *Patriarcha* (1680). According to Filmer, God granted to Adam, as the first King, an absolute and total political authority which was transmitted to his heirs. A divinely guaranteed monarch has absolute authority over his subjects, and is answerable, not to them, but to God. Locke finds the theory quite unworkable; for example, it cannot be used to justify any actual political authority, since it is impossible to show of any particular monarch that he is a genuine heir to Adam's original authority. The *Second Treatise* seeks to find some other more workable foundation for political authority. Though it does not deny that subjects do have a duty to God to obey their ruler, it insists that rulers are not absolute, and themselves have duties to their subjects. This means that if a ruler's commands did not deserve obedience, resistance to them might be justified.

Locke builds his theory on the idea of people living in a state of nature, in families and loose groups, without any political authority over them. His state of nature is not Hobbes's, for it is not composed of individuals following their natural instincts and living in fear of each other. Whether or not he does it, every person has a duty to God not to 'harm another in his life, ... liberty, ... or goods', and so has a parallel right to defend himself against such attack.

But if people have a right to their possessions, what makes them *theirs*? Why should a hut in which someone lives count as his? Why does the ground which a family happens to cultivate belong to that family? In Filmer's view, just as absolute political power was given to Adam by God, so the whole earth was given him too; hence, subjects have neither political power nor any right to property and possessions. Locke's response to this, his labour theory of property, is famous. For Locke, God made all men free and equal and set no one in power over them; similarly he gave to all men the earth and its fruits by which to support their life. This certainly means that Adam's heirs cannot be alone in having a right to private property, but in saying this, it does not explain how such a right arises in the first place. By itself, this denial of Filmer's view could entail a theory of communal property. Locke further explains, therefore, why one man should have a right to this land and these crops, another to that. The land someone cultivates is necessarily *his*: this is simply a special case of the fact that each man unquestionably has a right to his own life and labour, and so has the right to the products of that labour. 'Whatsoever then, he removes out of the state that nature hath provided, and left it in, he hath mixed his labour with, and joined to it something that is his own, and thereby makes it his property.'

Even though people in the state of nature have rights and duties concerning the lives, liberty, and possessions of themselves and others, it does not follow that these are respected and obeyed. Perhaps they will be unclear in the complexities of particular cases. Perhaps, too, someone may lack the power to defend his rights, or he may go too far in his own defence. Having these possibilities in mind, people agree to unite, and to 'enter into society to make one people, one body politic, under one supreme government'. They leave the state of nature 'by setting up a judge on earth with authority to determine all the controversies and redress the injuries that may happen to any member of the commonwealth'. This does not mean that they put themselves into the hands of an absolute authority. Unlike Hobbes, Locke believes that people under an absolute authority are not really in civil society; effectively they are still in a state of nature, for they may need to defend their rights against that authority. The judge of Locke's civil society is not absolute, but answerable to 'the will and determination of the majority' in his dealings with individual rights and duties. The views and wishes of the majority form a court of appeal against the decisions of their ruler. For Locke, 'the consent of any number of freemen capable of a majority' produces the continuing existence, as well as the actual beginning, of any political society.

Locke faces the objection that there is no historical evidence for his account of the creation of political authority. Certainly, no present authority could be justified by appeal to any such explicit consent. People are simply born into civil societies, and come under their laws and authority without choice. His answer depends on a distinction between tacit and explicit consent. By remaining in society, one gives one's tacit consent to it. His suggestion that one is always 'at liberty to go and incorporate himself into any other community, or to agree with others to begin a new one ... in any part of the world, they can find free and unpossessed' has been ridiculed, and is even less plausible now than when he made it. But his whole account can perhaps be understood so as to avoid such objections. Given its basic anti-absolutist thought that, whether within or without political society, men have a right to life, liberty, and possessions, it can be seen as a kind of picturesque metaphor which, in explaining the structure of legitimate political authority, reveals it to be based on the consent of the governed.

The notion of tacit consent gains further plausibility when one sees that a possibility of legitimate resistance or revolution follows from the idea that the ultimate basis of authority is the 'will and determination of the majority'. For this means that 'the community perpetually retains a supreme power of saving themselves from ... their legislators, whenever they shall be so foolish, or so wicked, as to lay and carry on designs against the[ir] liberties and properties'.

Locke is anxious to defend his political philosophy against the accusation that it *encourages* rebellion. Even the doctrine that political power is divinely given may not, in the particular circumstances of some cruel tyrant, actually prevent rebellion. Moreover, whatever one's account of political power, no one would urge a revolution 'upon every little mismanagement in public affairs'. But the question of *when* rebellion or revolt is justified needs an answer. Unsurprisingly, Locke's is that 'The People shall be Judge'.

In 1692 Locke's Irish friend, William Molyneux, recommended the *Essay concerning Human Understanding* to the Provost of Trinity College, Dublin. 'So wonderfully pleased and satisfied' was he with it that, as Molyneux wrote to Locke, 'he has ordered it to be read by the Batchelors in the College, and strictly examines them in their progress therein'; and so it came about that Locke's masterpiece was on the curriculum which faced George Berkeley, the subject of the next chapter, when he entered Trinity as a student in 1700.

7

George Berkeley (1685–1753)

George Berkeley was born near Kilkenny in Ireland in 1685.
He studied languages, mathematics, and philosophy at Trinity
College, Dublin, where he became a Fellow in 1707. He was
ordained into the Anglican Church in 1710. In his early travels to
London he met various intellectuals and literary people such as
Joseph Addison, Alexander Pope, and Jonathan Swift. In the
1720s, having become disillusioned with what he saw as a decline
in the moral and spiritual standards of European culture, he
formed the project of founding a college in Bermuda for the
sons of English settlers and natives, both from Bermuda and the
American mainland. With a Royal Charter, and parliamentary
approval, he left in 1728 for America. Having reached Newport,
Rhode Island, he decided to start the college there, but, despite
promises, financial support was not forthcoming, and he returned
to England. In 1734 he was appointed Bishop of Cloyne, eventually moving to Oxford in 1752, where he died the next year. His
Bermuda project, his attempt to develop tar-water as a cure for
the dysentery which followed the hard Irish winter of 1739–40,
and his evident concern for his parishioners, were all born of a
kind and generous character. According to Pope he had 'ev'ry
virtue under heav'n', while his wife said that 'humility, tenderness,
patience, generosity, charity to men's souls and bodies, was the
sole end of all his projects, and the business of his life'.

Berkeley's ideas were formulated early. His *Essay towards a
New Theory of Vision* was published in 1709, and was followed
the next year by his master-work, *A Treatise concerning the Principles of Human Knowledge*. Despite its readability the *Principles*,
as it is known, was neither well received nor, in Berkeley's view,
properly understood. Consequently he attempted more explanation of its doctrines in his *Three Dialogues between Hylas*

and Philonous (1713). He wrote also on the theoretical bases of the sciences of motion (*De Motu*, 1721) and mathematics (*The Analyst*, 1735). In common with his central philosophical works, these are imbued with religious belief and feeling, something which is explicitly the subject in his *Alciphron* (1732).

Berkeley's philosophy marks the turn of the tide against the world picture which had developed in the seventeenth century, and which had reached one of its classical expositions in Locke's *Essay*. Though he did not reject the methodology and interests of the 'new philosophy', nor attempt to go back beyond it to some earlier view, he thought that, in allowing too much to materialism, philosophy had taken a wrong turn. As in Gassendi and Locke, the 'new philosophy' was often anti-sceptical in intent, and its advocates were often not complete materialists, in that they genuinely thought to find room for religion, God, and the soul. Berkeley, nevertheless, thought that to concede anything to materialism was to concede too much, and that any element of materialism inevitably led to scepticism and, atheism. In a sincere attempt to display the importance of God in the scheme of things, Berkeley sought to rebuild the 'new philosophy' on the more solidly religious foundations of a complete and thoroughgoing spiritual immaterialism.

According to the standard seventeenth-century view, there exist, independently of and antecedently to our perception of them, material bodies. Given the distinction between primary and secondary qualities, such material things are not quite as they appear; unlike their extension, their colour (for example) is nothing but an ability, stemming from their atomic or corpuscular constitution, to cause certain ideas in our minds. According to some, this material world was all that exists. For Hobbes there is no *immaterial* God, nor are there *immaterial* souls or minds. God and minds do exist, but materially so. Thinking and perceiving, which might naturally be attributed to an incorporeal mind, are simply complex motions in matter. But most of those who thought there was a material reality were not uncompromising materialists of a Hobbesian sort. Most of them believed in an immaterial reality too. Though Locke does allow the possibility that matter might think, he tends to the view that we do have immaterial minds; and for him there certainly is an immaterial God. For many in the seventeenth century this immaterial God was an important part of their whole world-view. He not only created the material world but also, like a divine watchmaker, set it going by an initial injection of motion, and kept it going by occasional adjustments.

Like many others, Berkeley objected to the complete materialism of Hobbes. But he was equally unhappy with the typical alternative, with what he saw as the uneasy combination of materialism and immaterialism. It failed to allow God his proper place, and was really no better than complete materialism. It ultimately led, he believed, either to scepticism about the very existence of the world or, by quite misunderstanding God's relation to that world, to atheism or complete materialism. At least Hobbes was consistent for, as Berkeley noted, 'Matter once allow'd, I defy any man to prove God is not matter'.

The uneasy combination of materialism and immaterialism, which in Hobbes is resolved into a complete materialism, is resolved by Berkeley into a complete immaterialism in which God has a role far more crucial than in the standard seventeenth-century view. Starting with the more usual anti-Hobbesian belief in an immaterial God and perceiving minds or souls, he went one step further and said that this is all there is. He took this to be a truth 'so near and obvious to the mind, that a man need only open his eyes to see' it. All the 'furniture of the earth, . . . all those bodies which compose the mighty frame of the world', he says, 'have not any subsistence without a mind.' If they 'do not exist in my mind or that of any other created spirit, they must either have no existence at all, or else subsist in the mind of some eternal spirit.'

Startlingly bold as this idea is, the arguments for it were initially contained in just the first thirty-three short sections of the *Principles*. Berkeley wrote more fully in the *Three Dialogues*, but this work was unfortunately hardly better understood than the *Principles* itself. The basic problem he encountered was getting across why his own complete immaterialism was not itself more overtly and explicitly sceptical than the standard view that there exist both material bodies and incorporeal minds or spirits. Since, as the very titles of his books illustrate, his immaterialism was explicitly and primarily put forward as an antidote or corrective to scepticism and atheism, it was important that he explain this. The *Principles* is subtitled as an inquiry into the grounds of 'Scepticism, Atheism, and Irreligion'; according to its preface it will be useful 'particularly to those who are tainted with scepticism, or want a demonstration of the existence and immateriality of God, or the natural immortality of the soul'. The *Three Dialogues* aims to demonstrate 'the incorporeal nature of the soul, and the immediate providence of a Deity: in opposition to Sceptics and Atheists'.

According to Berkeley, the usual combination of materialism and immaterialism leads to scepticism because of its 'supposing a difference between *things* and *ideas*'. Once a distinction is made between our perceptions of material things and those things themselves, 'then are we involved all in *scepticism*'. For it follows from this distinction that we see only the appearances of things, images of them in our minds, not the things themselves, 'so that, for aught we know, all we see, hear, and feel, may be only phantom and vain chimera, and not at all agree with the real things'.

One person who clearly distinguished mental ideas and material things in this way was the French Cartesian, Nicolas Malebranche. According to Malebranche, in his *Search after Truth* (1675), we do not see material things in the world directly. The 'immediate objects' of our minds are 'ideas'. When we see the sun, he says, the 'immediate object' of our perceiving mind is not the sun itself 'but something that is intimately joined to our soul, ... an *idea*'. When we perceive an object there is an idea of it 'present to' our mind. But it is possible that we have such an idea when there is no external thing like it. 'It often happens [as in dreams and fevers] that we perceive things that do not exist.'

Against the background of this account of perception as something *indirect*, with ideas figuring as intermediaries between our minds and material things, Malebranche discusses what reason we have for our usual supposition that the material world exists at all. Descartes had thought that its existence could be demonstrated on the basis of God's goodness. God would not give us ideas and perceptions which inevitably lead us to suppose a world, unless there actually was one. But Malebranche rejected various parts of Descartes's proof, concluding that theoretically the material world was no more than a possibility, and could be accepted only on the basis of faith. This obviously reintroduces the scepticism which Descartes had hoped to avoid, and it increases when Malebranche goes on to argue that our perceptions of a material world could not anyway be caused by that world even if there were one, but must be caused by God. This, as Berkeley comments, is 'a very precarious opinion'. It supposes 'without any reason at all, that God has created innumerable beings that are entirely useless, and serve to no manner of purpose'. Malebranche makes the material world not just a bare possibility but a redundant one too.

Besides finding the seeds of scepticism about a created world in Descartes and Malebranche, whose theories of perception involved both material things and ideas, Berkeley found them in Locke too. He also found that Locke, once having made a similar distinction, provided no good reason for belief in a world over and above the ideas we have of it. Unlike Descartes, who felt the need to prove their existence, and Malebranche, who was certain he could not, Locke simply had no doubt that material things existed and caused our ideas: 'The actual receiving of ideas from without ... makes us know, that something doth exist at that time without us, which causes that idea in us.' But he was completely unsure how matter could affect mind, and Berkeley fastened on this. If we cannot understand how body 'should imprint any idea in the mind', our having such ideas 'can be no reason why we should suppose matter or corporeal substances, since that is acknowledged to remain equally inexplicable with, or without this supposition'.

The scepticism towards which, in Berkeley's view, much seventeenth-century philosophy implicitly tended, is not unrelated to the traditional Greek scepticism which was brought to light in the sixteenth century. The arguments rehearsed by Sextus Empiricus purported to show that, because perception of secondary qualities such as tastes and colours varied from person to person, we cannot know how things really are in respect of these. But in the seventeenth century some philosophers, such as Descartes and Malebranche, had extended this to saying that tastes and colours

are, like pains, simply subjective modifications, and are not properties of material objects after all. Malebranche had argued, moreover, that the argument from the relativity of perception was just
as applicable to primary qualities such as extension and motion:
what looks small to me will seem large to a mite; some movements
may be too slow for the human eye to detect. Because of his
Cartesianism, Malebranche could not go so far as to say that
material objects were not really extended or in motion, but Pierre
Bayle had argued that such restraint was unjustifiable. In his
Dictionary (1697), Bayle points out that although the 'new philosophers' do not set out to be sceptics, they go even further in
extending sceptical arguments to the conclusion that smells, colours, and tastes, 'are perceptions of our soul and that they do not
exist at all in the objects of our senses'. But, asks Bayle, why
not go further still? Why cannot the same thing be said about
extension? 'Why could not an entity that had no extension be
visible to us under the appearance of ... extension?' Perception
of extension is subject to relativities too, the same thing appearing
to be different shapes according to our view. So it is not by 'their
own real or absolute extension that bodies present themselves to
our minds', and we have no reason not to conclude that 'they are
not extended in themselves'.

From his reading of Descartes, Locke, Malebranche, and
Bayle, Berkeley had become sensitive to, and appalled by, the
sceptical tendencies of the new philosophy. He might have rejected Malebranche's extension of the arguments about relativity
of perception from secondary to primary qualities; he might have
rejected the further conclusions Bayle said should be drawn from
them. But, with some appearance of paradox, he does not.
Instead, he wholeheartedly takes them over: they show up materialism as an inadequate position and leave the way open for
his spiritual immaterialism, with God at its centre. He would have
preferred it had their arguments led directly to immaterialism,
and showed not merely that we do not know what qualities material objects have, but indeed that they have none, or even that
there are no such objects. But although by themselves they do
not take us this far, they do at least point the way. They do show
that primary qualities, as we experience them, are on an equal

footing with secondary qualities, and are simply perceptions or ideas in the mind. Why not, then, take the hint and cut through the sceptical problems the arguments invite, boldly saying that if all we know are ideas, then ideas are all there are? Faced with the evidently troublesome distinction between things and ideas, Berkeley in effect collapses it; he concludes that *ideas are things*. As he explains, 'Those immediate objects of perception, which according to [some] ... are only appearances of things, I take to be the real things themselves.' This is not to say that there are ideas and *no things*: that would be the ultimate scepticism. What he proposes is to change 'ideas into things'; and to do this is *not* to deny the existence of a world of things. Certainly, he is denying the world of the philosophers, a world of objects beyond direct perception. But he is not, he claims, denying the world of common sense, not denying the reality of a world of directly perceived objects. Given the distinction, between ideas and things, which leads to scepticism, is it not wisest, asks Berkeley, to say that our ideas *are* things, 'to trust your senses, and laying aside all anxious thought about unknown natures and substances, admit with the vulgar those for real things, which are perceived by the senses'?

But Berkeley's claims that his Immaterialism avoided the scepticism endemic in his predecessors, and restored philosophy to the beliefs of sound common sense, were not accepted. His view that there is no reality other than minds or spirits, and their ideas, was taken to be scepticism run riot. All Berkeley's arguments, according to Hume, 'though otherwise intended, are, in reality, merely sceptical'. To Leibniz he was 'The Irishman who attacks the reality of bodies ... [and] belongs to the class of men who want to be known for their paradoxes'. Saying that he ought to be able to get through a closed door as easily as an open one, Swift is supposed to have left him standing on the doorstep. Dr Johnson begged a Berkeleian not to take his leave from the group he was with, 'for we may perhaps forget to think of you, and then you will cease to exist'.

Berkeley robustly denied all this. 'We are not for having any man turn *sceptic*, and disbelieve his senses; on the contrary we give them all the stress and assurance imaginable; nor are there any principles more opposite to scepticism, than those we have laid down.' He is not, he says, one who 'detracts from the existence or reality of things'; and anyone who thinks otherwise 'is very far from understanding what hath been premised in the plainest terms I could think of '. It is possible, however, that Berkeley's evident sensitivity to charges of scepticism is rooted not simply in his cherished hope that they are false, but also in some dim feeling that they are not completely unjust. For indeed they are not, and it is understandable that they should have been made.

His proud boast is that 'the same principles which at first lead to *scepticism*, pursued to a certain point, bring men back to common sense', and that rather than being a purveyor of wild and new paradoxes, he has 'unite[d] and place[d] in a clearer light that truth, which was before shared between the vulgar and the philosophers'. What he has done, he explains, is to combine the belief of his philosophical predecessors that 'the things immediately perceived, are ideas which exist only in the mind' with the common-sense belief that 'those things ... [we] immediately perceive are the real things'; and these two, put together 'do in effect constitute the substance of what I advance'. But because he accepts *something* from the philosophers' view, a view which leads to scepticism, he himself runs the risk of it. Even though he does accept common-sense beliefs, he also accepts something from the philosophers which common sense would not. With those he attacks he shares the premiss that all that we are directly aware of are ideas, which have no existence apart from a perceiving mind. In doing so he diverges from common sense. He is right to insist that he rejects the material world of *philosophers*, such as Descartes and Malebranche, a world which is only indirectly perceived *via* our ideas. This clearly is all he *wants* to reject. But in agreeing with the philosophers that all that we know are ideas, he runs the risk of rejecting altogether any real world. The non-philosophical 'vulgar' do not think that all that we know are ideas. Berkeley's desire to support non-sceptical common sense, while accepting from the philosophers something common sense would not, gives an awkward complexity to what he says.

Berkeley sees that, to his identification of mental ideas with real things, 'it will be objected that we see things actually without or at a distance from us, and which consequently do not exist in the mind'. The point that in dreams we see things 'as existing at a great distance' indicates that this objection can be answered, but he acknowledges that some explanation is needed. Indeed, it was a consciousness of this problem that led to his earlier book, *The New Theory of Vision*. Its conclusions are, in fact, more limited than those of the *Principles*. They apply only to sight, and leave the reader assuming that, unlike what we see, what we touch exists independently of the mind. But Berkeley already had his more general immaterialism in mind. He saw the problem of *visual* perception as a particular difficulty for it, and, wishing to proceed gradually, he intended the *New Theory* to prepare the way for the *Principles*. The *New Theory* has two explicit aims: to reach an understanding of how objects can be perceived by sight as having size, position, and arrangement in space; and to discuss the differences between sight and touch.

Distance, says Berkeley, must be perceived by the mediation of something else for, 'being a line directed end-wise to the eye', it is not perceived 'of itself'. It had been held that we 'judge of distance' as we do 'a conclusion in mathematics ... by virtue of geometry and demonstration'. According to the science of optics, light travelling from objects enters the eyes at differing angles according to distance; the further away an object is, the more nearly parallel are the light rays from it. Diagrams illustrating this are familiar from books on optics, and the idea was that distance is calculated and judged by means of these angles. Berkeley denies that we go in for such calculations in judging distances. We are not aware of these lines and angles of theoretical geometrical optics; they cannot be the intermediary by which we perceive distance. What the intermediary is is awareness of our eye-movements. According to distance, different eye-movements are required for focusing on different objects.

Berkeley infers from this that, lacking experience of such eye-movements, a blind man who gained sight 'would, at first, have no idea of distance by sight; the sun and stars ... would all seem to be in his eyes, or rather in his mind'. He argues further that what we see, 'the immediate objects of sight', are not things in space at a distance from us, but ideas in the mind. Our visual world is an immediately present one of colours and flat two-dimensional shapes. When we say that what we see is a mile away, we must mean that were we to move forward a mile, we would be 'affected with such and such ideas of touch'; and so Berkeley concludes that the things we see are not the same as those we touch. In the case of hearing and touch this is clear; strictly speaking, what we hear is not a coach in which we might travel, but rather its noise. The same goes for the coach we see. 'A man no more sees and feels the same thing than he hears and feels the same thing.'

Having explained judgements of distance, Berkeley turns to judgements of size. Since what we see is not what we touch, and since the former are ideas in the mind, which change in size as we move forwards to some thing, the actual size he is concerned with must be that of the tangible object. This, he says, is judged on the basis of the size, distinctness, and vigorousness of the visible object. We learn from experience that certain visible appearances are connected with tactile objects of a certain size at a certain distance from us.

Distance and size, says Berkeley, are seen in the way that 'we see shame or anger in the looks of a man'; though invisible themselves, these feelings are 'let in by the eye along with colours and alteration of countenance, which are the immediate objects of vision'. Moreover, just as the connection between certain looks and shame is one which we learn solely by experience, 'without which ... we should no more have taken blushing for a sign of shame than of gladness', so is the connection between certain visual experiences, and distance and size.

For Berkeley, then, what we see and what we touch are different things. Visual size is not tactile size, visual extension and motion are not tactile extension and motion. Why then, it will be asked, do 'visible extension and figures come to be called the same name with tangible extension and figures, if they are not of the same kind with them'? Visible ideas are signs and indications of tangible ideas, and have a constant and universal connection with them which was 'learnt at our first entrance into the world; and ever since, almost every moment of our lives, it has been occurring to our thoughts, and fastening and striking deeper on our minds.' It is no wonder that what we see becomes identified with, and spoken of as if it were the same as, what we touch.

The connection between the visible and the tangible is conceived by Berkeley as having been set up by God. 'The proper objects of vision constitute an universal language of the Author of Nature, whereby we are instructed how to regulate our actions in order to attain those things that are necessary to the preservation and well-being of our bodies.' Experience teaches us which tangible objects to expect after certain visible objects. This 'visual' language is of immense use. A sighted person can make predictions about the future course of tangible experience—falling over a precipice or hitting a wall—which to a blind man 'seem as strange and unaccountable as prophecy doth to others'.

The *New Theory of Vision* explicitly teaches that what we see is not what we touch, and exists only in the mind, not in an external space. But what of the mode of existence of tangible objects? The quite unambiguous teaching of the *Principles* is that they, too, are mind-dependent ideas. All objects, such as trees, stones, and books, whether in their tangible or visible aspects, are such that their '*esse* [their mode of existence] is *percipi* [to be perceived], nor is it possible they should have any existence, out of the minds or thinking things which perceive them'.

Though the upshot of Berkeley's theory is relatively easy to grasp, what he says in its support is somewhat inadequate. Consider, he says, that when we speak of the existence of a sensible thing we mean that we *are* perceiving it by various of our senses, or *could* perceive it were we suitably placed. 'The table I write on, I say, exists, that is, I see and feel it; and if I were out of my study I should say it existed, meaning thereby that if I was in my study I might perceive it.' This might seem reasonable enough. It allows that the existence of a sensible thing need not consist in its *actually being perceived* but, rather more weakly, in its *being perceivable*; in allowing this it would certainly be more acceptable to common sense. But it hardly supports the conclusion which, without further ado, Berkeley draws from it: that it is not possible that sensible things 'should have any existence out of the minds or thinking things which perceive them'. According to this, the existence of sensible things consists solely in their *actually being perceived*. That the argument will not do as it stands is, in fact, conceded in the *Three Dialogues*, where Berkeley allows Hylas to make the point that, although the existence of a sensible thing might consist in its *being perceivable* (as in the premiss), it does not (as in the conclusion) consist in it *actually being perceived*. Berkeley, therefore, gets his spokesman, Philonous, to add that, since the only *perceivable* things are ideas, and since they exist only when *actually* being perceived, it follows that sensible perceivable things are ideas, and do exist only when actually being perceived. This further move does indeed strengthen the argument, but does not sit happily with Berkeley's original remark about the un-perceived desk in the unoccupied study.

In another argument Berkeley suggests that it would be a 'manifest contradiction' to suppose that sensible things might exist 'unperceived' or 'distinct from ... being perceived by the understanding'. He uses three premisses: that houses, mountains, and rivers are what we perceive by sense; that what we perceive by sense are 'our own ideas or sensations'; and that ideas cannot exist unperceived. He concludes from these that houses, mountains, and rivers cannot exist unperceived. Given that 'ideas' are things which, like sensations and feelings, are essentially mind-dependent, the third premiss is something with which the philosophically sophisticated would agree; it is, too, something with which the vulgar, if persuaded to consider the matter, could easily be brought to agree. The second, Berkeley says, is 'evident'. No doubt it would have been so to Descartes, Malebranche, and Locke: *they* might have agreed with Berkeley that what we perceive are ideas. But it would hardly have been so to the 'vulgar'. What would have been evident to them, of course, is the first premiss; so, although Berkeley's surprising conclusion follows validly from his three premisses, these are not all equally acceptable both to the 'philosophers' and to the common sense of the 'vulgar'. Though accepting both the first and the third, the philosophically unsophisticated would reject the second. Berkeley's predecessors, on the other hand, would accept both the second and the third, and reject the first. The 'contradiction' in thinking that things might exist 'distinct from ... being perceived by the understanding' is 'manifest' neither to the philosophers nor to vulgar common sense.

Despite his claim that he does not make things into ideas but only ideas into things, the feeling remains, as, in effect, Berkeley concedes, that 'all that is real and substantial ... is banished out of the world', and that everything has been made into 'so many chimeras and illusions on the fancy'. He proceeds to show, therefore, that with only ideas at his disposal, he can nevertheless distinguish between reality and illusion. There is, he says, 'a *rerum natura*, and the distinction between realities and chimeras retains its full force—[even though] they both equally exist in the mind, and in that sense are alike *ideas*'. He points out that sometimes we have control over our ideas, and sometimes not: often we can set ourselves to imagine what we want; at other times, however, as in broad daylight, 'it is not in my power to ... determine what particular objects shall present themselves to my view'. Furthermore, it happens that our ideas are sometimes 'more strong, lively, and distinct' than at others. Berkeley does not elaborate on this second point, but presumably is gesturing towards the difference between actually experiencing something, such as heat, and remembering or anticipating it. Finally, ideas sometimes have a 'steadiness, order, and coherence' and come in 'a regular train or series': 'when we perceive by sight a certain round luminous figure, we at the same time perceive by touch the idea or sensation called *heat*.' Berkeley uses these three facts about ideas to distinguish 'ideas of sense' from 'ideas of imagination'. Perception of reality is a matter of having 'ideas of sense', which have the characteristics of being involuntary and not subject to our control, of being strong and lively, and of having a coherence and order. Illusions, dreams, and fancies, on the other hand, consist of 'ideas of imagination' which are voluntary and subject to our wills, and which lack both lively strength and orderly coherence. It appears to have escaped Berkeley's attention that not all imaginary things, for example a drunkard's pink rats, are voluntary and lack the vivacity of the real thing, and also that, when I set myself to imagine something, I can make my ideas as orderly and coherent as I like.

It is interesting to note that his three criteria for distinguishing reality from illusion can be found also in the works of those philosophers, such as Descartes and Locke, whose view he rejects. Unlike Berkeley, they held that there are both ideas and a world of things which cause them. But this does not mean that they did not face the troublesome question Berkeley faces, of how to distinguish between illusion and reality. They still needed to explain when those ideas were faithful perceptions of a real world, and when not. For them, however, the involuntariness, vivacity, and coherence of certain ideas is evidence that they are *caused by* real things; for Berkeley it means they *are* real things.

The notion of our sometimes involuntarily having ideas in coherent series, continues the *New Theory of Vision*'s doctrine that God has established connections between the ideas of sight and those of touch. Unlike the voluntary 'ideas of the imagination', which are the product of our own will, the involuntary 'ideas of sense' are produced in us by God. Their being excited in us in an orderly fashion 'gives us a sort of foresight, which enables us to regulate our actions for the benefit of life'; and this testifies to God's wisdom and benevolence. Berkeley's seventeenth-century predecessors were as anxious as he was to suggest that the regularity of nature is a manifestation of God's goodness; but in making an independent material world the cause of ideas, they give God a less crucial role than Berkeley does.

The uneasy feeling that, despite his claim to make things out of ideas, Berkeley has 'banished all that is real and substantial out of the world', can be articulated by suggesting that, whatever philosophers might want to say about 'real things', common sense will want to speak about them in ways which, at least at first sight, are not licensed by their being constructed out of ideas. Ideas, it seems, cannot be made into things, because various truths about them are not suitable for transmutation into truths about things. According to Berkeley, real things are dependent on, and do not exist outside of, perceiving minds; according to common sense, however, they are independent of our perception of them. It does, therefore, seem to follow from Berkeley's view, that 'bodies are annihilated and created every moment, or exist not at all during the intervals between our perception of them'. It is true that, by contrast with those that constitute 'imaginary things', the ideas that constitute 'real things' *are*, for Berkeley, independent of the human mind: they are not subject to the voluntary control of the mind that perceives them. But, at least to begin with, this is not sufficient. Pains are not subject to our will, we do not choose to feel them, but this does not lead us to say that they have an existence independent of our experience of them. Something more of the requisite independence could be achieved by Berkeley's doctrine that ideas which are not subject to our own will are produced in us by God: the independence of a real thing, its having some continuity despite interrupted perception of it, could be explained in terms of a continued readiness on God's part to excite the requisite ideas in us at suitable moments.

But although God does have the role in Berkeley's philosophy of accounting for the continued perceivability of real objects apart from our actual perception of them, it is not quite in the way we have just described. So keen is Berkeley on the idea that the existence of real objects consists in their *actually* being perceived, that he appears to explain their continuity, not by a readiness on God's part to excite ideas *in us*, but rather by God's *own* continued perception. 'When I deny sensible things an existence out of the mind, I do not mean my mind in particular, but all minds. ... There is therefore some other mind [i.e. God's] wherein they exist, during the intervals between the times of my perceiving them.' And *this* explanation fails to solve a further problem. Besides having a continuous existence independent of perception, the real things of common sense are *public*. Not only do I suppose that the desk in my study exists when neither I nor anyone else is there to perceive it, I also suppose that I, and everyone else, can perceive the *same* desk. Berkeley's making of ideas into things needs to do justice to the thought that we all (including God, for Berkeley) perceive the same things. If the continuity of real things consists in their actual perception by God, in what does their publicity (to us, and also to God) consist? Berkeley's account of continuity seems unable to explain publicity in any way sufficiently akin to that of the perception-independent world of vulgar common sense.

Given his belief that the idea that objects exist independently of a perceiving mind contains 'a manifest contradiction', one might expect Berkeley to provide some explanation of why anyone should mistakenly have it. He goes some way towards doing this in terms of what he calls 'the doctrine of abstract ideas'. According to this, we can have, for example, an idea of colour *alone and as such*, an idea abstracted from any thought of particular extended things with their particular colours. It thus lends support to the materialistic view that it makes sense to think of objects in abstraction from a mind which perceives them. Can there be, Berkeley asks, 'a nicer strain of abstraction than to distinguish the existence of sensible objects from their being perceived, so as to conceive them existing unperceived'? So sure is Berkeley of the ultimate impossibility of this abstraction that he even says that he will let his whole case rest on it. Why cannot one think of 'sensible things' such as trees and tables apart from their being sensed? 'Surely there is nothing easier than to imagine trees ... in a park ... and nobody by to perceive them.' According to Berkeley, this does not show that he is wrong. One can indeed imagine a tree without anyone perceiving or having ideas of it, but in imagining it *one is oneself* having ideas of it. 'The mind, taking no notice of itself, is deluded to think it can and doth conceive bodies ... without the mind.' Despite Berkeley's comment that 'a little attention' to this will enable anyone to see how successfully it makes his point, this argument has provoked a considerable amount of detailed discussion.

In Berkeley's view, the mistaken doctrine of abstraction is also involved in the distinction between primary and secondary qualities, a distinction which he rejects along with the materialism it involves. It cannot be, he says, that 'figure, motion, and the rest of the primary or original qualities do exist without the mind ... [while] colours, sounds, heat, cold, and such like secondary qualities ... are sensations existing in the mind alone', for 'extension, figure, and motion, abstracted from all other qualities, are inconceivable'. Primary qualities must, therefore, be 'where ... the other sensible qualities are ... to wit, in the mind and nowhere else'.

In the Introduction to the *Principles*, Berkeley spends a considerable time arguing against the doctrine of abstract ideas. This is justified by his belief that abstractionism does more than obscure the truth of immaterialism. The 'Principles' of his title are those 'of Human Knowledge', and what motivates his objection to materialism is that it leads to scepticism and atheism. Materialism is a 'false principle' which 'stay[s] and embarrass[es] the mind in its search after truth'; it raises specious problems, it draws us 'into uncouth paradoxes, difficulties, and inconsistencies, which multiply and grow upon us as we advance in speculation'. Now although Berkeley pictures the doctrine of abstraction as a support of the 'false principle' of materialism, it is additionally a 'false principle' in its own right. 'Besides the external existence of the objects of perception, another great source of errors and difficulties, with regard to ideal knowledge, is the doctrine of *abstract ideas*.' Directly and of its own accord, it has 'not a little contributed towards spoiling the most useful parts of knowledge': 'the plainest things in the world, those we are most intimately acquainted with, and perfectly know, when they are considered in an abstract way, appear strangely difficult and incomprehensible.'

The doctrine of abstract ideas stems from a concern with what, when it was debated in the Middle Ages, was called 'the problem of universals'. Though Berkeley's interest in the problem connects with his immaterialism, he is continuing a discussion to which not only the Aristotelians, but also Hobbes, Gassendi, and Locke, made contributions. It will be convenient, therefore, to make some mention of their views on the matter.

These views concern the fact that the singular particular things which we can point to and pick out with the words 'this' and 'that', and to which we often give names, such as 'James' or 'John', are not thought of as being *merely* particular. Like many other particulars, James and John are both men; 'this' and 'that' may both be triangles. What, then, is the mode of existence of these general 'universals', such as 'man' or 'triangle'; and how do they figure in our knowledge and thought? How, that is, do they relate to the particular things which are instances of them, and to our minds when we think of those things *as* men, or *as* triangles?

According to 'realist' theories, such as those of Plato and Aristotle, besides the particular things we perceive, there are 'universals' which are essentially general. For Plato these 'universals' were located as ideal Forms in an abstract world which was accessible to our intellect and thought. The particular things of the perceptible world 'partook' or 'shared' in them. According to the less extreme realism of Aristotle and many of his followers, 'universals' were dependent for their existence on sensible particulars, which 'embodied' them, often as their 'forms' or 'natures'. A particular man is some matter with the general form of humanity 'impressed' on it. By a process of 'abstraction', moreover, it was possible for these general notions to be 'impressed' on our minds or intellects, thus making it possible for us to think in terms of them.

In the Middle Ages such realist theories were often denied. There are, it was said, no essentially general entities, whether existing apart from particular things, or embodied in them. All things that exist are particular and singular. At times this anti-realism took the form of an extreme nominalism, according to which the words 'man' and 'triangle' are general only in that they are used of a number of different things. There is no general nature in common to those things, and any idea we have is never general or abstract, but always of some particular thing. On this view, the generality of the word 'man' is no different from that of 'John' which, after all, can itself be used of a number of things. At other times the anti-realism took a conceptualist form, according to which universality is a matter of our ideas or concepts. Though all things that exist in the extra-mental world are particulars and singular, it is nevertheless possible for us to form essentially general or abstract ideas.

Hobbes was certainly an avowed anti-realist. For him there was 'nothing in the world universal but names; for the things named are every one of them individual and singular'. But whether he was a pure or consistent nominalist is unclear. He does say that the word 'universal' is 'never the name of any thing existent in nature, nor of any idea or phantasm found in the mind'. When 'man', 'stone', or 'living creature' is said to be 'universal', we are not to understand that 'man, stone, etc. ever was or can be universal, but only that these words, "living creature", "stone", etc., are *universal names*, that is, names common to many things.' Thus the name 'man' is simply a name used for a number of particulars, and any idea of 'man' is always an idea of some particular man, and simply reminds us of other particulars. Yet it is not arbitrary that the idea of this particular should remind us of these and not other particulars, and that these and not the other particulars should have the same name used of them. 'One universal name is imposed on many things, for their similitude in some quality.' This reference to similitude is suggestive of realism, in its invocation of some common, shared, universal property.

Gassendi was an anti-realist too. In answer to 'obscure and spurious questions such as whether universals may exist by themselves, whether they are only in the mind, whether they exist separate from things or only with them', he says that these 'great universals are nothing more than ... common nouns ... that can be applied to more than one object'. He agrees, then, with what he ironically calls 'that mad opinion', that there is 'no universality outside of thoughts or names'. Unlike Hobbes, however, he allows that ideas or concepts can be general, universal, or abstract, and need not be of particulars. He talks of forming 'the universal concept of a man from having seen Plato, Socrates, and others'. He speaks, too, of properties which Plato and Socrates 'share', and of their 'similarity' to each other, and this again seems to reintroduce an element of realism.

Locke's views on this matter are similar to Gassendi's, but are developed at greater length. How, he asks, 'come we by general terms, or where find we those general natures they are supposed to stand for?' Unlike Hobbes, he does not think that words are general by being collective names for a number of particulars; 'they do not signify a plurality.' They are general by being 'made the signs of general ideas'. As for these general ideas, ideas of particular things, they come to be general by our 'separating from them ... [any detail] ... that may determine them to this or that particular existence'. Thus, the abstract 'idea' of 'man', what Locke calls a nominal essence, differs from that of 'Peter' and 'Paul' 'in the leaving out something, that is peculiar to each individual; and retaining so much of those particular complex ideas, of several particular existences, as they are found to agree in'. For Locke, then, 'general words signify ... a sort of thing'; and they do this by being a sign of an abstract idea or nominal essence in the mind, 'to which idea, as things existing are found to agree, so they come to be ranked under that name; or ... be of that sort'. In urging against the Aristotelian realists that 'general and universal, belong not to the real existence of things; but are the inventions and creatures of the understanding', he is, of course, reaffirming from a different angle his rejection of their 'forms', and their talk of the possibility of there being 'real' definitions of things. Though Berkeley mentions the scholastics, 'those great masters of abstraction', it is Locke on whom he particularly focuses in his criticism of abstract ideas.

'Whether others have this wonderful faculty of *abstracting their ideas*', he ironically says, 'they best can tell.' For his part, he cannot 'abstract one from another, or conceive separately, those qualities which it is impossible should exist so separated'. He cannot form an idea of extension *as such*, which is 'neither line, surface, nor solid, nor has any figure or magnitude but is an idea entirely prescinded from all these'. He cannot 'frame a general notion by abstracting from particulars' to form an 'abstract idea' of 'man' 'wherein, it is true there is included colour, because there is no man but has some colour, but then it can be neither white nor black, nor any particular colour; because there is no one particular colour wherein all men partake'.

For Berkeley, an idea must be an idea of a particular, a particular line, or a particular man. This means that ideas cannot be *abstract*, but it does not mean that they cannot be *general*. A general *use* can be made of ideas of particulars. The idea of a particular line can be 'made to represent or stand for all other particular lines of the same sort'. A justification for talk of abstract ideas is that it provides an explanation of how our thought and knowledge can be general; 'how we can know any proposition to be true of all particular triangles, except we have first seen it demonstrated of the abstract idea of a triangle.' Berkeley's suggestion that particular, non-abstract ideas can be general in their use enables him to do this. Geometrical demonstrations which prove something to be true of all triangles do not do so by proving it to be true of an abstract triangle to which all triangles correspond. 'The idea I have in view whilst I make the demonstration' may be of a *particular* right-angled triangle with sides of a certain length, but I may, nevertheless, be sure that it holds of all right-angled triangles if, by not mentioning the ways in which it differs from them, I use this one to stand for them all. Though 'the diagram I have in view' includes particular details, 'there is not the least mention made of them in the proof of the proposition'.

In what ways have the false doctrine of abstraction, and the equally mistaken materialism to which it lends support, been a 'great source of errors and difficulties' in our search for knowledge? What 'disputes and speculations, which are esteemed no mean parts of learning, are rejected as useless' by the adoption of correct principles of knowledge? Berkeley remarks that the opinion that words like 'good' and 'happiness' 'stand for general notions abstracted from all particular persons and actions' has 'rendered morality difficult, and the study thereof of less use to mankind'. He also points out, in passing, that various questions of the sort which have cropped up in earlier chapters of this book, such as whether matter can think, and how it produces mental sensations, 'are entirely banished from philosophy' by the adoption of immaterialism. He says rather more, however, about their ill effects on natural philosophy, mathematics, and religion.

So far as natural philosophy, the first of 'the two great provinces of speculative science, conversant about ideas received from sense', is concerned, the confusion engendered by materialism is great. As Berkeley points out, sceptics 'exaggerate, and love to enlarge on' that part of the seventeenth-century picture of the world according to which independently existing material things have a real essence of which we are ignorant. 'We are miserably bantered, say they, by our senses, and amused only with the outside and show of things.' Given Berkeley's immaterialism, however, the idea that things have real essences (be they scholastic forms or corpuscular constitutions), which are the cause of their properties, simply has no place. Natural philosophy should not be thought deficient because we are ignorant of the ultimate causes of the characteristic properties and regular behaviour of things. Such uniformities and regularities are not part of an independent material world, but simply a matter of what ideas God excites in our minds. They are not 'the result of any immutable habitudes, or relations between things themselves, but only of God's goodness and kindness to men in the administration of the world'. Since there are no natures or essences, there is nothing closed to natural philosophy. It can do all there is for it to do, which is to discover regularities among our God-given ideas, and to systematize these in the most useful way. In Chapter 5 we saw how natural philosophers, such as Boyle, tried to defend themselves against charges of encouraging materialistic atheism by suggesting that, since the natural world is God's creation, the study of it leads towards, not away from, things spiritual. An argument of this kind seems much more plausible when proposed by Berkeley; it no longer seems like special pleading when set against the background of his God-centred, immaterialist view of the natural world.

Berkeley offers Newton's achievements in illustration of how the hidden rules, or 'laws of nature', by which God excites ideas in us can be discerned and systematized. Newton was sufficiently imaginative to see not only that 'there is something alike' in the falling of a stone and the rising of the tides, but also that all bodies 'have a mutual tendency towards each other'. Berkeley believes, however, that Newton's presentation of his theories in his *Principia* or *Mathematical Principles of Natural Philosophy* (1687) were flawed by his tendency to abstractionism. The talk of *absolute*, as well as relative, time, motion, and space, wrongly supposes 'those quantities to have an existence without the mind', and conceives them in abstraction from our observations.

Mathematics is the second of 'the two great provinces of speculative science' to which Berkeley turns his attention. He is forthright in his view that its practitioners, too, are involved in 'the errors arising from the doctrine of abstract ideas, and the existence of objects without the mind'. His worry is not that these errors undermine any of their actual results: 'that the principles laid down by mathematicians are true, and their way of deduction from those principles clear and incontestable, we do not deny.' It is, rather, that the errors that they make permeate their philosophy of mathematics, their account of its foundations, of what their subject is about, and in what direction it should develop.

Arithmeticians fail to see that the function of numerical symbols and signs is to enable us to deal in general ways with groups of particular sensible things. They think, instead, that they stand for 'abstract ideas of *number*', which they take to be the province of their subject. This misconception has meant that their work has not been 'subservient to practice', and able to 'promote the benefit of life'. It has meant that it has been 'abstracted from ... all use and practice', and has become a purely speculative matter of 'high flights and abstractions'. Since numerals do not stand for 'numbers in abstract' but for 'particular things numbered', the misguided interest in the properties of such abstractions has really been a trifling concern with mere language or formalism.

As for geometers, their work is misdirected not only, as in arithmetic, by a false belief in abstract ideas, but also by the erroneous materialism that the 'objects of sense exist without the mind'. For these mistakes have led to the belief that *extension*, the subject-matter of geometry, is infinitely divisible, a belief 'thought to have so inseparable and essential a connection with the principles and demonstrations in geometry, that mathematicians never ... make the least question of it'. In its turn, this belief has led to 'geometrical paradoxes', and is 'the principal occasion of all that nice and extreme subtility which renders the study of *mathematics* so difficult and tedious'.

According to Berkeley, however, finite extension is not infinitely divisible, and any problems and questions which rely on its being so are spurious. Any particular finite extension is simply an idea in our minds, and cannot have more parts than the finite number we perceive it to have. It is only when one supposes that, as well as such ideas, there is either 'extension in abstract' or extended, external, material things which might have parts we cannot perceive, that one might come to believe in the infinite divisibility of finite extension.

For Berkeley, human knowledge must be concerned either with ideas, or with the minds or spirits which perceive them; for apart from these there is nothing. Mathematics and natural philosophy are concerned with ideas, and Berkeley now turns from them to spirits, of which God is a special case. We have been thought to be 'ignorant of the nature of spirits', he says, because we have no 'idea' of spirit. In fact, however, our knowledge here is not so deficient as has been imagined. It is, indeed, true that we do have no 'idea' of spirit. It is 'manifestly impossible there should be any such *idea*', for we can have no sensory experience of spirits. They are active things which perceive, think, and will, and these properties cannot be represented in a passive idea. But this does not mean that the words 'soul', 'spirit', or 'spiritual substance' are meaningless. In the *Dialogues* Berkeley shows awareness of the possible accusation of unfair dealing: he admits 'spiritual substance; although [we] ... have no idea of it', while he denies that 'there can be such a thing as material substance, because [we] ... have no notion or idea of it'. His reply is that we have no idea of material substance because matter is an impossibility and could not exist; whereas, though we can have no sensory idea of spiritual substance, minds are not an impossibility and could exist. Indeed, one knows by reflection that one's own soul or mind does exist.

Though Berkeley offers little explanation of this last claim about our *own* minds, he says more about our knowledge of the existence of other minds. Both other spirits like ours, and God, are known 'by their operations, or the ideas by them excited in us'. Spirits are not perceived by sense; they are not ideas but things which have ideas. But we do perceive people's *bodies*, and these behave in such a way as to show that they are accompanied by 'a distinct principle of thought and motion [i.e. a mind] like to ourselves'. It is in a similar way that the existence of God is revealed to us. The only difference is 'that whereas some one finite and narrow assemblage of ideas denotes a particular human mind, whithersoever we direct our view, we do at all times and in all places perceive manifest tokens of the divinity'.

At the end of the *Principles*, Berkeley reminds us that his 'main drift and design' has been to 'inspire my readers with a pious sense of the presence of God'. His success in this depends directly on the success of his immaterialism, for it is obvious how it continually points the way towards God. Though there are some things which 'human agents are concerned in producing', it is plain that 'the works of Nature, that is, the far greater parts of the ideas or sensations produced in us, are not produced by, or dependent on, the wills of men'. They must be produced by some other spirit, and if we attend to their 'constant regularity, order, ... magnificence, beauty, and perfection', we see that they must be produced by an 'eternal, infinitely wise, good, and perfect' spirit, which is God. Materialism, on the other hand, leads us away from God. It leads either to problems about the relation between God and the world (for example, to a denial that it is His creation) or, as in the case of 'Epicureans, Hobbists, and the like', to the attempt to reduce everything to matter. 'How great a friend material substance hath been to *atheists* in all ages, were needless to relate. All their monstrous systems have so visible and necessary a dependence on it, that when this corner-stone is once removed, the whole fabric cannot choose but fall to the ground.'

According to David Hume, the subject of the next chapter, Berkeley's account of abstract ideas was 'one of the greatest and most valuable discoveries that has been made of late years in the republic of letters'. Berkeley held, as we have seen, that an abstract general idea is simply an idea of a particular thing used to stand for other such ideas; and it is clear that what Hume applauds is Berkeley's refusal to accept any ideas other than those of immediate and concrete experience.

It is just this denial of anything beyond what is directly given in experience that marks Berkeley out as an empiricist. His attempt to identify the real world of perceived objects with our perception of it, and his denial of any experience-independent material reality, are the most obvious examples of this. But his account of natural philosophy, which rejects any inner mechanisms or real essences 'hid ... behind the scenes' which would purport to explain 'those appearances which are seen on the theatre of the world', is a clear example too. Indeed, just as Berkeley's immaterialism foreshadows the phenomenalist theory of perception developed by the so-called Logical Empiricists of this century, so his view, according to which the aim of science is not to provide explanations of nature's regularities but only to arrive at concise and useful descriptions of them, foreshadows their instrumentalism.

Despite Berkeley's claim that 'we do at all times and in all places perceive manifest tokens of the divinity', the important place occupied by God in his philosophy will inevitably seem as far removed from immediate experience as the material world of seventeenth-century philosophy seemed to Berkeley. We should not forget, however, that Berkeley's own commitments are to God rather than to the predetermined demands of some idealized empiricism.

8

David Hume (1711–1776)

David Hume was born in Edinburgh in 1711, into a Calvinist family. His childhood and some of his later life was spent on the family estate near Berwick. He attended Edinburgh University where he studied classics, mathematics, and philosophy. He was expected to become a lawyer, but by about his eighteenth year he had set his sights on a life of writing and philosophy. He composed the *Treatise of Human Nature* in his early twenties in France. Though now considered one of the great works in philosophy, it made little mark when it was published in 1739 and 1740; according to Hume's own account it 'fell dead-born from the press'. His youthful hopes were further dashed in 1745 by his failure, a result of his move away from Calvinism, to obtain the Chair of Ethics and Pneumatical Philosophy at Edinburgh University, an institution which now houses its philosophy department in a building named after him.

The publication, in 1748, of *An Enquiry concerning Human Understanding*, a more lively, popular, and easily accessible version of Book 1 and some of Book 2 of the *Treatise*, began to win him a measure of the reputation he desired. But neither this nor the rewriting of Book 3 of the *Treatise* as *An Enquiry concerning the Principles of Morals*, prevented his failure in 1752, to become Professor at the University of Glasgow. He provoked hostility from the orthodox by various writings on religion, such as the *Natural History of Religion* (1757), a work in which he argues that Christian monotheism arises out of negative emotions such as a subservient desire to flatter. This hostility led him to keep his *Dialogues concerning Natural Religion* from publication until after his death, but it did not prevent his eventually achieving, on the basis of his six-volume *History of England* (1756–61), the reputation he sought. His years in Paris, where he served as assistant to the English ambassador from 1763, saw him a social lion, idolized and sought after. The last years of his life were spent in his native Edinburgh, where he died in 1776.

Though it was only later in life that Hume had much favourable public reputation, he was always greatly loved by his friends. A kind and considerate man, he was quite evidently an entertaining companion, endowed with wit and charm. The value he placed on benevolence, kindliness, and the uplifting effects of good humour, is plain from his writings. But his sharp remarks about gloomy 'monkish virtues', and the 'dismal dress' in which many have clothed morality, seem partly directed against a darker side of his own nature which his philosophizing unfortunately did nothing to help. His genuine benign sociability was, perhaps, not so much a matter of natural cheerfulness as something he successfully strove to achieve.

A prime concern of seventeenth-century philosophy had been the idea of a science of the natural world. Hume's main concern is with extending such a science to man, to produce what was sometimes called 'moral science'. Indeed, he says, we need to become clear about human nature before we can become clear about the sciences in general, for they all have a relation to it. Undreamt-of improvements might occur in them, given knowledge of 'the extent and force of human understanding'. A study of human nature is more clearly relevant to logic, morality, and politics (which deal with our reasonings, feelings, and associations with each other), than it is to mathematics, natural philosophy, and religion. But though these latter do not study man, they are studied by him. We might understand them better if we understood our own understandings of them. 'There is no question of importance, whose decision is not comprized in the science of man; and there is none, which can be decided with any certainty, before we become acquainted with that science.' Hume's plan is to 'march up directly' to the centre of all the sciences, to human nature itself. In attempting 'to explain the principles of human nature, we in effect propose a compleat system of the sciences, built on a foundation almost entirely new'.

But if the science of man, 'moral science', is the foundation of all the other sciences, what is *its* foundation? Referring to Bacon's achievement of putting natural philosophy on a firm basis by making it 'experimental', Hume says that the only solid foundation we can give to his science of man is to see it 'laid on experience and observation'. The *Treatise* is subtitled 'An attempt to introduce the experimental method of reasoning into moral subjects', and in it Hume proposes 'the application of experimental philosophy to moral subjects'. Since the principles of any science must be founded on the authority of experience, we must 'glean up our experiments' in the science of man. Hume does not merely pile up observations about the phenomena of the human mind. He is conscious that first appearances are often deceptive, and that one should formulate and test hypotheses. He devises 'experiments to confirm ... [his] system', and his desire to follow what he sees as the methods of natural philosophy is constantly evident.

Despite the reference to Bacon as the first to introduce 'experimental reasoning' into natural philosophy, Hume's real hero is his near-contemporary Newton, who advocated the older Paduan method of resolution and composition. In his *History of England* he refers glowingly to 'the greatest and rarest genius that ever rose for the ornament and instruction of the species', and his procedure: 'cautious in admitting no principles but such as were founded on experiment; but resolute to adopt every such principle, however new or unusual.' Newton's great achievement was to formulate the principle of gravitation, according to which material bodies attract each other in inverse proportion to the square of their distance apart, and in direct proportion to their masses. This principle related and brought together a number of diverse facts and observations, and Hume attempts to find principles which will give similar coherence to a variety of mental phenomena. Just as Newton made systematic sense of the movements of the planets, Hume proudly makes sense of apparently disparate activities of the mind. On occasions, Hume's parallel between himself and Newton runs even closer. Three of his systematizing 'principles' concern the way various of our ideas become associated, and here, says Hume, 'is a kind of *attraction* which in the mental world will be found to have as extraordinary effects as in the natural, and to show itself in as many and as various forms'. Hume further applauds Newton for his reluctance to speculate about the ultimate causes of gravitational attraction; like Locke, Hume thinks that gravity, cohesion of the parts of matter, and communication of motion by impulse, are in the end 'totally shut up from human curiosity and enquiry'. A similar modesty is appropriate in the moral sciences; we must be content with finding some systematizing principles, and restrain the 'intemperate desire' to inquire into their causes. They are best left as '*original* qualities of human nature, which I pretend not to explain'.

Hume's 'science of man' falls into three parts, according as it deals with 'the understanding', 'the passions', or 'morals'. There is a tendency to treat him as an epistemologist whose concern is primarily with 'the understanding', but he states at the outset that the passions are his real interest. In his account of these, he points out that they have marked analogies with beliefs as already explained in connection with 'the understanding'. Given his conception of the systematizing procedures of the natural sciences, he naturally argues that this shows that he is on the right lines. But the historical development of his ideas probably followed the reverse route to this. In his actual development, it would seem, his epistemology gained support from his moral psychology, and not contrariwise as he implies. His account of the passions and moral sentiments, according to which they are all a matter of reactive feeling and emotion rather than of reason, was greatly influenced by Francis Hutcheson. Hume seems to have realized the possibility of giving a similar account of beliefs and the understanding. His final, unified picture of us is of creatures whose thoughts, feelings, and moral valuations are all governed by the same principles of our own nature. Neither our factual beliefs and thoughts nor our moral sentiments are set apart, or different, from our reactive emotions and feelings. All alike are the inevitable result of the same observable features and principles of human nature, a nature which is essentially no different from that of any other animal.

The tendency to take Hume to be primarily concerned with the understanding, the topic of Book 1 of the *Treatise* and of the *First Enquiry*, goes along with supposing that the important introductory first sections of these works relate only to it. In fact, the apparatus he sets up there permeates all three parts of his 'science of man'.

Hume is concerned throughout with what he calls *perceptions*, a general term for the contents of our minds such as sensations, beliefs, judgements, memories, and feelings, both moral and otherwise. Hume gets the term from Hutcheson, preferring it to Locke's term 'idea', which he thinks is used too broadly for its proper meaning. Locke's informal recognition of a difference between 'ideas' as we first get them in sensation, and as they occur in memory, imagination, or thought, is more sharply marked by Hume as a division of 'perceptions' into 'impressions' and 'ideas'. 'Impressions', he says, are 'all our sensations, passions, and emotions, as they make their first appearance in the soul'; 'ideas' are 'the faint images' of these in thinking, reasoning, memory, and imagination. 'Everyone will readily allow, that there is a considerable difference between the perceptions of the mind, when a man feels the pain of excessive heat ... and when he afterwards recalls to his memory this sensation.' The difference between the two is supposed to be one of degree, not of kind. It is one of 'vivacity' or 'liveliness': impressions are lively perceptions, ideas are simply less vivid copies of these. But there is a difficulty in this which Hume hardly recognizes. If an idea of anger is simply a less vivid perception than the impression which is anger itself, it would seem that to remember being very angry is to be mildly angry. Of course, our memories might revive our anger; but they need not, and, in any case, remembered anger is not anger itself. In fact there are at least two ways in which Hume is untrue to his official story that the difference between ideas and impressions is simply one of degrees of liveliness. First, his principles of association of ideas are different from those for impressions, a difference left quite unexplained by reference to varying vivacity. Secondly, ideas are said to combine additively, like lengths or numbers, whereas impressions are said to mix, like colours.

An important empiricist feature in Gassendi and Locke was the view that all our ideas are derived from experience. This view reappears in Hume. But whereas for them it is a considered theoretical claim about how things must be, it is put forward by Hume more as an *observation*. Consideration of the mental phenomena of ideas and impressions, in particular of the fact that the former are simply less 'vivid' copies of the latter, suggests to Hume, as a hypothesis to be tested, that 'all the perceptions of the mind are double, and appear both as impressions and ideas', so that for every impression there is a resembling idea, and for every idea an impression which it copies. Further observation shows that the hypothesis needs amendment. One does sometimes have ideas without impressions, and impressions without ideas. One could imagine a never-experienced city with golden pavements and ruby walls; and, conversely, a city one has seen may not be remembered in all its detail. Accordingly, Hume distinguishes, as did Gassendi and Locke, between *simple* and *complex*, and allows that we can imagine what we have never experienced so long as we have experienced the relevant parts. Thus he limits his hypothesis of a correspondence between ideas and impressions to the case of simples. In support of this more limited claim he points out that blind men, incapable of colour impressions, have no colour ideas, and suggests that we perform the experiment of analysing our thoughts or ideas to test their reducibility to simple ideas, which are copied from experienced impressions. 'Those who would assert that this position is not universally true ... have only one, and that an easy method of refuting it; by producing that idea, which, in their opinion, is not derived from this source.'

The *Treatise* puts forward the correspondence and resemblance of ideas and impressions as a basic principle of human nature which will be of great use in further investigations. It 'is the first principle I establish in the science of human nature'. But the *Enquiry* brandishes it in a rather more provocative way, as a weapon to banish unintelligible jargon and rectify confused reasoning about abstruse topics. If we suspect 'that a philosophical term is employed without any meaning or idea (as is but too frequent) we need but enquire, *from what impression is that supposed idea derived*? And if it be impossible to assign any, this will serve to confirm our suspicion.' The first of these uses of the principle is less threatened than the second by Hume's mention of one 'contradicting phenomenon': given experience of an interrupted range of shades of blue, it may not be impossible, he thinks, to form an idea of the missing shade. Hume's principle that any term, in order to be meaningful, must be associated with some experienced impression has been much applauded by philosophers in this century, and is one of the things responsible for his classification as an empiricist.

Locke divided experience, the source of all our ideas, into *sensation* and *reflection*. In a similar fashion, Hume distinguishes perceptions into impressions of sensation and those of reflection. There are important differences, however. For Locke, ideas of reflection are got by the notice 'the mind takes of its own operations' about ideas of sensations; examples are the ideas of 'perception', 'thinking', and 'believing'. For Hume, following Hutcheson's amendments to Locke, perceptions of reflection are secondary impressions, such as hopes and fears, which are caused in us by sensations, such as pleasures and pains. These Humean impressions of reflection were classed by Locke as modes of the sensations of pleasure and pain.

If impressions and ideas of sensation cause impressions of reflection, what is *their* cause? Why do these make their 'appearance in the soul' in the first place? Hume does not care much about this, as he is more interested in sensory impressions and ideas, and their effects *once we have them*. He does speak of their arising from 'the application of objects to the external organs', but though, unlike Locke, he thinks that there need be no special mystery as to why events in the material world should have mental effects, the physical details of this are for the physiologist to find. He also speaks of their arising from 'unknown causes' which are 'perfectly inexplicable by human reason'; and what he has in mind here is the sort of metaphysical question which concerned Malebranche and Berkeley: the question whether they are produced by an external world or by God. Again, though, this is not 'material to our present purpose'. This refusal to interest himself in questions which go beyond the immediate facts of experience is a further empiricist strand in his thought.

Besides there being a correspondence between simple ideas and the antecedent impressions which they copy, it sometimes happens, as in the case of memories, that the *order* and *combination* of our ideas corresponds to the order and combination of their original impressions. At other times, however, as in imagination and thought, there is no such corresponding order. Nevertheless, Hume argues, there must be some principle or principles governing the order of the ideas of imagination and thought. Newton's gravitational force associates the planets and sun together; there must similarly be 'a gentle force', 'a kind of *attraction*' which groups our ideas. No one, says Hume, has attempted to formulate any such 'universal ... uniting principle', but he can discern three. The first is a matter of 'resemblance': 'our imagination runs easily from one idea to any other that *resembles* it; ... this quality ... is to the fancy a sufficient bond and association.' Thus, in Hume's example, a picture naturally leads our thoughts to what it pictures. The second concerns proximity or 'contiguity in time or place': when someone mentions a certain room we are naturally led to think of other parts of the same house. The third is that of 'cause and effect': the thought of a wound leads us to thoughts of the pain which it caused. Of these principles of association of ideas, there is none 'which produces a stronger connection in the fancy, and makes one idea more readily recall another' than the third.

Are there any similar principles for association of impressions? For impressions of *sensation* Hume would presumably say there are. In our experience of snow there is often an association of impressions of coldness and whiteness; and the reason for this lies partly in the physiology of perception, partly in facts about snow. But any inquiry into this would be the business of natural, and not moral, science; the 'examination of our sensations belongs more to anatomists and natural philosophers than to moral'. The impressions of *reflection*, however, those secondary impressions which are caused not by objects acting on our senses, but by perceptions of sensation, *are* Hume's business. Indeed, since they are what constitute our passions and moral sentiments, they are what 'principally deserve our attention'. Hume finds just one principle which governs their association, and this is 'resemblance'. The passions of love and benevolence resemble each other in being pleasant, and are apt to lead to each other. In the course of his detailed study of the phenomena of human nature, Hume discovers further organizing and systematizing principles, but those of association are all that emerge from his initial general scene-setting.

It is against this background that Hume approaches his main concern: our 'passions, desires, and emotions'—the last two parts of the tripartite study of human nature, and the topics of Books 2 and 3 of the *Treatise*, and of the *Second Enquiry*. But these impressions of reflection are secondary to the ideas (and impressions) of sensation which are their causes and which, as a consequence, must be investigated first. Ideas of sensation, then, are the topic of the first part of moral science which concerns 'the understanding'—for thinking, reasoning, knowledge, and belief, are concerned with ideas.

In the *First Enquiry*, Hume first observes about the 'understanding' that 'all the objects of human reason or enquiry' divide into two; a division which is closely related to Locke's distinction between 'knowledge', and 'belief' or 'opinion'. On the one hand there are *relations of ideas*, the intuitively or demonstratively certain propositions of geometry, algebra, and arithmetic. He agrees with Locke that these are 'discoverable by the mere operation of thought'. Pythagoras' theorem, that the square of the hypotenuse of a right-angled triangle equals the sum of the squares of the other two sides, expresses a relation between various ideas. We need not go beyond ideas to see, as in a demonstration, that that theorem is true; our ideas remaining the same, we cannot conceive it false. *Matters of fact*, on the other hand, such as that the sun will rise tomorrow, are neither intuitively nor demonstratively certain. This belief about the sun does not depend on relations between our ideas, so there is nothing unintelligible or self-contradictory about the thought of its not rising. Any matter of fact and its opposite are conceivable 'with the same facility and distinctness'.

Hume finds no problem in our believing various relations of ideas. They are intuitively or demonstratively obvious and it is impossible to conceive of them not holding. But what, he goes on to inquire in great detail, 'is the nature of that evidence which assures of any ... matter of fact?' Why do we have the belief that the sun will rise tomorrow, and not the equally intelligible belief that it will not? Our ideas are not related in such a way as to rule this out as a contradiction. Some beliefs of 'matters of fact' raise no problem: they are based on the 'present testimony of the senses', or 'the records of our memory'. I believe that the sun *is* rising because I see it doing so; I believe that it *rose yesterday* because I saw and remember it. But what of my belief that it *will* rise tomorrow? This goes beyond memory or present sense-experience, and since it is no more intuitively or demonstratively certain than a belief to the contrary, there is room for some explanation of why I have it, rather than its contrary.

Though there is no intuitive or demonstrable relation between the ideas of the sun and of its future rising, they quite evidently are associated in my mind; and they must be so, it seems, by virtue of at least one of the three principles of association of ideas which Hume has to hand. The requisite principle must be one which takes us from the impressions or ideas of my present experience and memory to some further supposed fact, and the only one of the three that does this is that of cause and effect. Why do we believe 'any matter of fact, which is absent', for example, that our friend is in France? The reason given will always be some other present fact or memory with which it has a causal connection, a letter received from him, or a memory of his plans. Hume concludes, therefore, that 'all reasonings concerning matters of fact seem to be founded on the relation of Cause and Effect. By means of that relation alone we can go beyond the evidence of our memory and senses.' Having satisfied himself that 'the nature of the evidence' that assures us of matters of fact has to do with the associative principle of cause and effect, Hume proceeds to 'enquire how we arrive at the knowledge of cause and effect'.

The *Treatise* and the *First Enquiry* proceed somewhat differently here. The attempt of the former, which is to understand the *idea* of cause, and hence to find the *impression* from which it is derived, is made only incidentally in the *Enquiry*. There Hume first reconvinces himself that the cause–effect relation really is not an a priori relation between ideas, and that 'matters of fact', which have to do with that relation, really are distinct from the intuitively or demonstratively certain propositions of arithmetic and geometry. Causes and effects, he argues, 'are discoverable, not by reason but by experience'. Without experience, and on the basis of his 'rational faculties' alone, Adam could not know that water would drown him. From our ideas, taken in themselves, we can have no knowledge of causes and effects. It is not conceivable that three times five is not equal to half of thirty; but it is conceivable (that is to say, there is no a priori contradiction in the thought) that an unsupported stone will not fall.

'Matters of fact', then, such as that this stone, left unsupported, will fall, *are* different from 'relations of ideas'; our belief about the stone is based on past experience, not on a priori reasoning. Satisfied on this point, Hume presses the inquiry further. Precisely how does that belief relate to past experience? Why should past experience 'be extended to future times' in this way? After all, it is one thing to say that 'such an object has always been attended with such an effect', and quite another to say that 'other objects, which are, in appearance, similar, will be attended with similar effects'. Some explanation is needed of why we infer from the one to the other.

It would seem, says Hume, that we have 'the supposition that the future will be conformable to the past': from 'causes which appear *similar* we expect similar effects'. But quite how does this supposition figure in our minds? How exactly does it relate our past experience to our expectations for the future? One possibility is that we use it as a premiss in an argument. Perhaps we take as one premiss, 'our past experience has been of such and such a sort', add to it as a second premiss, 'the future will be like the past', and then conclude 'our future experience will be of such and such a similar sort'.

If the supposition we seem to make, 'the future will be like the past', functions in this way, as a premiss in a piece of demonstrative reasoning about matters of fact, then it must itself be a 'relation of ideas', or a further 'matter of fact'. On the one hand, however, just as it is not an a priori matter of relations between ideas that we believe that this unsupported stone will fall, so it is not an a priori matter that the future will be like the past. There is no purely a priori reason, rooted in the nature of our ideas themselves, that the future really will be like the past. There is 'no contradiction [in saying] that the course of nature may change'. On the other hand, however, it cannot simply be a further matter of fact. For what would the nature of our reasoning concerning *it* be? If belief in some matter of fact, which goes beyond present experience and memory, is a result of an argument which depends on the premiss, 'the future will be like the past', then that premiss, if itself a matter of fact, would, in its turn, have to be the result of a similar argument. It would, says Hume, 'be evidently going in a circle' to explain our beliefs in matters of fact in this way. So our past and present experience is not related to our expectations for the future by means of a piece of reasoning which has as a premiss, 'the future will be like the past'. In moving from past instances of a certain sort to similar future instances, we are not 'engaged by arguments'. This conclusion is unavoidable on general grounds too: 'the most ignorant and stupid peasants—nay infants, nay even brute beasts' are surely not led from their past experience to expectations about the future 'by any process of argument or ratiocination'. Either, then, we must give up the idea that the supposition that the future will be like the past is relevant to our forming beliefs about particular future matters of fact, or we must find some alternative account of the way in which this supposition figures in our minds.

Hume's alternative is as ingenious as it is simple. The observation that, in forming beliefs about the future, we seem to be proceeding on the supposition that the future will be like the past is, when properly understood, simply the observation of an effect that 'custom and habit' have on our minds. The mental move, from noticing that 'such an object has always been attended with such and such effects' to expecting that 'other objects, which are, in appearance, similar, will be attended with similar effects' is not a move of reason. It is the manifestation of a mental habit which has grown up as a result of that past experience. That there is such a habit of mind is, Hume says, a principle we must just accept. But the general idea is perfectly reasonable. It is quite familiar that the repetition of any particular act 'produces a propensity to renew the same act'.

This principle of mental habituation explains why the idea of a stone being left unsupported should be associated in my mind with the idea of its falling. It also explains why, when I see or have the impression of a stone about to be left unsupported, I should have the *idea* or thought of its falling. But why, in this latter case, should I form the *expectation* of its falling? Why should I *believe* it will? What, indeed, is a belief or expectation, as opposed to a mere idea or thought? According to Hume, beliefs are enlivened, vivacious ideas. They are not as lively as impressions, of course; after all, a belief that something is happening, or will happen, is not an actual impression of its doing so. But they are more lively than mere ideas or thoughts. Why then, to repeat the question, should my mental habits, together with the present impression of a stone about to be left unsupported, lead to the *belief*, the *enlivened* idea, that it will fall? Hume's answer is simply that the vivacity of that impression carries across to the associated idea, enlivening it, and transmuting it from a mere idea or thought into a belief or expectation. The belief in any unobserved matter of fact is a result of both mental custom and a present impression.

Having found in many instances, that ... flame and heat, snow and cold ... have always been conjoined together; if flame or snow be presented anew to the senses, the mind is carried by custom to expect heat or cold, and to *believe* that such a quality ... will discover itself upon a nearer approach.

The conclusion is, then, that our 'matter of fact' beliefs which go beyond the present testimony of the senses are not the result of reasoning. We do not believe that this stone will fall because the idea of its not doing so is a priori incompatible with the idea of its being left unsupported, or because we add to the fact that similar stones have fallen in the past the premiss 'the future will be like the past'. We believe it as the result of seeing the stone left unsupported now, and of a habit formed by seeing stones fall in the past. This conclusion is highly significant for Hume. It means that our 'matter of fact' beliefs are things that form in us as a result of principles which are constitutive of our own nature, rather than things we actually form for ourselves. Such a belief

is the necessary result of placing the mind in such circumstances. It is an operation of the soul, when we are so situated, as unavoidable as to feel the passion of love, when we receive benefits; or hatred when we meet with injuries. ... [Such beliefs are] a species of natural instincts, which no reasoning or process of the thought and understanding is able either to produce or prevent.

The interpretation of 'matter of fact' belief as 'a species of natural instincts', as something which is more properly 'an act of the sensitive, than of the cogitative part of our natures', is one of the distinctive features of Hume's philosophy. It is the result of applying to the 'understanding' the kind of view he got from Hutcheson about moral judgements; for these, we shall see, are taken by Hume to be matters of reactive feeling and emotion, as opposed to reason.

It will be useful here to consider Hume's relation to the tradition of scepticism which had been a feature of philosophy since the mid-sixteenth century. Is Hume's view about our 'matter of fact' beliefs a manifestation of scepticism? In arguing first that they are not based on reason and argument, and then going on to explain how they result from custom, habit, and associative mechanisms in our minds, is he saying that, although we undoubtedly have such beliefs, they are quite unwarranted and unjustified? It might be said that he is not, and that he has no interest in the question whether our beliefs are *justified* or not; his interest is solely the *descriptive* one of how they come about. After all, when he discusses our belief in the external world in the *Treatise*, he explicitly says that the question is not *whether* the belief is true, but *why* we have it. It is commonly supposed, however, that Hume *is* being sceptical when he argues that these ordinary 'matter of fact' beliefs (as also our beliefs in the external world, and in a continuing personal identity) are not based on reason: he *is* arguing that these beliefs are *unjustified*. Correct though this view may be, it is not so obvious that his explanation of how these beliefs arise from habit and various principles or mechanisms of human nature, is meant as a reinforcement of the sceptical claim that they are unjustified. On the contrary, this explanation seems intended as a response to the challenge of sceptical arguments which he himself endorses. How is this so?

According to the Pyrrhonian sceptics, we ought to suspend judgement on all matters. Such a suspension of judgement was, it was recognized, somewhat impractical, so, while casting doubt on our abilities to attain knowledge, they added that one must live one's daily life by the common beliefs and customs of one's society. Earlier chapters have observed the responses of Bacon, Gassendi, Locke, and Berkeley to such scepticism. In their different ways, and to different extents, they did not accept the sceptics' general suspension of judgement. Hume's response, embodied in his account of the generation of belief, is of a different sort. He does not say that there is *no need* for an overall suspension of judgement; after all, he finds nothing wrong with sceptical arguments. What he says is that such a suspension is *humanly impossible*. Human nature is so constituted that we cannot *choose* to suspend judgement on questions such as whether the sun will rise tomorrow. Correct as sceptical arguments are, for Hume they cannot lead us to give up our beliefs. Since our beliefs are not the product of reasoning, but the inevitable result of our mental constitutions, sceptical arguments cannot have this effect.

This is not to say that they have no effect. Pyrrhonian sceptics envisaged that their arguments, together with the consequent suspension of judgement on all matters, would lead to a calm peace of mind. In Hume's view they do quite the opposite; they do nothing but produce 'amazement and confusion'.

The *intense* view of these manifold contradictions and imperfections in human reason has so wrought upon me, and heated my brain, that I am ready to reject all belief and reasoning. . . . I am confounded with all these questions, and begin to fancy myself in the most deplorable condition imaginable, environed with the deepest darkness.

The view that sceptical arguments fail to convince despite their validity, because we *cannot* give up our beliefs, also explains why they 'amaze and confuse'. What else is to be expected from plausible arguments which run counter to beliefs formed as the inevitable effects of experience on our human nature? The antidote to such 'confusion' is simply to turn one's back on the arguments which produce it; dinner with friends and a game or two of backgammon are Hume's preferences. After this, the sceptical arguments cannot but seem 'cold, and strained'.

Despite all of this, however, Hume does not think that our beliefs are *all* equally natural and instinctive, and equally immune to sceptical argument. Sceptical arguments against some of them, in particular against many held by philosophers, such as a belief in 'substantial forms', may produce conviction. Amongst principles which might produce belief he distinguishes between those which are 'permanent, irresistible, and universal; such as the customary transition from causes to effects', and those which are 'changeable, weak, and irregular'. The first are

the foundation of all our thoughts and actions, so that upon their removal human nature must immediately perish and go to ruin; ... [the latter are] neither unavoidable to mankind, nor necessary, or so much as useful in the conduct of life; but on the contrary are observed only to take place in weak minds, and being opposite to the other principles of custom and reasoning, may easily be subverted by a due contrast and opposition.

Besides explaining the formation of our 'matter of fact' beliefs by reference to the associative principles of 'cause and effect', Hume also looks closely at the idea of 'cause'. Involved in it, he finds, is the idea of 'succession', for effects follow their causes; the idea of 'contiguity' in time and space, for unless 'linked by a chain of causes', effects are not distant from their causes; and finally, since causes are taken to *produce* their effects, the idea of some 'necessary connection' between the two. This last idea is certainly not the least important for Hume, and, putting the others aside, he tries to locate the impression from which it is derived. In his account of where it is *not* to be found, at least, Hume was influenced to a considerable degree by Malebranche.

There is no such impression of necessary connection in our experience of any particular cause and effect. When we see one billiard-ball causing another to move, all that 'appears to the *outward* senses' is a series of movements. The observation of a particular instance of a cause and its effect gives us no impression of 'any power or necessary connection; any quality, which binds the effect to the cause, and renders the one an infallible consequence of the other'. Perhaps, then, the idea is derived from the consciousness we have of our power over our own bodies? Hume thinks not. We are certainly aware that 'the motion of our body follows upon the command of our will', but it is equally certain that such a sequence simply presents itself to us as a brute fact, like the movement of one billiard-ball when struck by another. 'The power or energy by which this is effected, like that in other natural events, is unknown and inconceivable.' It would begin to appear that there is no impression to which our supposed idea of a connection between cause and effect can correspond. All events, whether within the material world or between our minds and the material world, 'seem entirely loose and separate'. We observe one thing following another, the movement of one ball following its collision with another, the movement of a hand following an act of will, 'but we never can observe any tie between them. They seem *conjoined*, but never *connected*.' Yet, if there is no impression there can be no idea, and our talk of connection between causes and effects must be meaningless nonsense.

There is, however, a further possible source of the idea: something related to a *constantly* observed conjunction of billiard-balls striking each other, as opposed to a single observed conjunction. After all, it usually happens that we begin to identify causal connections between events only after repeated experience. Moreover, we already know, from consideration of 'matter of fact' belief, that repeated experience of conjoined events leads to the establishing of a mental habit, such that a fresh impression of one of these events will lead to a belief or expectation about the other. Hume concludes that it is this expectation, the *feeling* of connection which we have as a result of mental habit, which constitutes the impression which is the source of our idea of causal connection. The 'connection ... which we *feel* in the mind, this customary transition of the imagination from one object to its usual attendant, is the sentiment or impression from which we form the idea of power or necessary connection.' In terms of what was said earlier, the impression of necessary connection is an impression of reflection. It is caused by the repetition of various impressions of sensation.

Hume's conclusion, that so far as the external objects which are causes and effects are concerned there is only constant conjunction, is brought to bear on the question of free will. According to the libertarians, in performing our actions we are at 'liberty' to do as we wish. According to the necessitarians, we are not free, but are subject to the same 'constraint' as the movements and operations of objects in the natural world. Undertaking what he calls 'a reconciling project', Hume argues that the disagreement 'has hitherto turned merely upon words'. Both sides agree that the objects in the natural world are under causal 'constraint', and all that they can mean, unless they are mistakenly to 'transfer the determination of thought to external objects, and suppose any real intelligible connection betwixt them', is that there is a regularity in their operations. But, as Hume illustrates, there is no difference, in terms of regularity and constancy, between the operations of matter and the voluntary actions of human beings. 'A man who at noon leaves his purse full of gold on the pavement at Charing-Cross, may as well expect that it will fly away like a feather, as that he will find it untouched an hour after.' The operations of natural bodies are no more 'constrained' than are human actions, for, apart from a tendency of the mind to form expectations about them, regularity and constant conjunction are all that exists; and human actions are no less constrained than the operations of natural bodies: 'The conjunction between motives and voluntary actions is as regular and uniform as that between the cause and effect in any part of nature.'

Hume carefully points out that this view of human action is not harmful to religion and morality. Indeed, he argues, it is essential to their support. Laws, both divine and human, are based on the supposition that there is a regularity between motive and action. Where there is not such a regularity, we do not praise or blame. Where actions 'proceed not from some cause in the characters and disposition of the person, who performed them, they ... can neither redound to his honour, if good, nor infamy, if evil'.

For Hume, the motivating causes in our characters and dispositions are passions, desires, and feelings. He argues that those who speak of 'the combat of passion and reason', and suggest that we ought to act according to reason are mistaken. Reason, he says, can never be a motive to action, and cannot oppose any desire in directing the will. This view is no surprise; if even our factual beliefs are not produced by reason, it is not to be expected that our actions are. By reason we may, Hume allows, work out how best to achieve our ends, how best to satisfy as many of our desires as possible, but beyond that it is impotent. 'Reason is ... only ... the slave of the passions, and can never pretend to any other office than to serve and obey them.' It is incapable of producing action or of 'disputing the preference with any passion or emotion'. In a famous sentence Hume says 'it is not contrary to reason to prefer the destruction of the whole world to the scratching of my finger'. The preference is a matter of feeling and passion. People mistakenly think, he says, that reason can be a direct influence on action, because they confuse it with 'calm passion', which can be. As he points out, what we commonly mean by 'passion' is 'a violent and sensible emotion of mind'. But (as we shall see below) passions and desires need not be violent; and when they are not, they may be mistaken for reason.

At the end of his investigation into 'ideas' and the 'understanding', Hume is ready to 'launch out into those immense depths of philosophy, which lie before me', and to undertake an investigation of impressions of reflection, those secondary impressions such as our passions, emotions, and moral sentiments which result from impressions and ideas of sensation. The perceptions which give rise to them are those of pleasure and pain; and this sometimes happens 'directly', as in the case of desire, joy, hope, and moral approval, sometimes 'indirectly' through the mediation of 'other qualities', as in the case of pride and love. The direct passions are further divided into the 'calm' and the 'violent'. Moral approval is a prime example of the so-called calm impressions of reflection, which are the topic of Book 3 of the *Treatise* and of the *Second Enquiry*. Desire is one of the 'violent' impressions. Violent direct passions, along with the indirect passions of pride and love, joy and hope, are the topic of Book 2 of the *Treatise*, and of its rather uninteresting summary in the *Dissertation on the Passions* (1757).

What Hume says about the violent direct passions is relatively straightforward. He speaks of them as arising from 'a natural impulse or instinct' which is 'perfectly unaccountable' as a fact about human nature. Desire and aversion, hope and fear, proceed directly from pleasure or pain. They are simple instincts towards or away from what is seen as 'pleasurable' (or 'painful'); they need no explanation by appeal to any other principles of human nature. 'The mind by an *original* instinct tends to unite itself with the good [which is pleasure], and to avoid the evil [which is pain].' Hume also mentions, in this category, the instinctive desires we might have to punish our enemies or give happiness to our friends, and our bodily appetites, such as hunger and lust.

Much more is said about the indirect passions of pride and humility, love and hatred, but it is possible to be brief about the main structure of Hume's account. Hume's 'pride' is not an unpleasant vice, as indeed it is not when we talk of 'taking a pride' in something; conversely, his 'humility' is best understood as 'shame', that emotion which we feel when we are ashamed of something. All of these emotions have an *object*: some other person, in the case of love and hatred, ourselves in the case of pride and humility. It is not that when we are proud we are necessarily proud *of* ourselves. We may be proud of our children, or of our country. The point is that we are proud of *our* country, not of *other people's*. When we are proud, 'whatever other objects may be comprehended by the mind, they are always considered with a view to ourselves'. But the idea of ourselves or of others cannot be the *cause* of these passions. Pride and humility, love and hatred, are not caused by the mere idea of ourselves or of others. Pride is caused by some quality of something considered as being related to ourselves, such as the beauty of our country; love is caused by some quality of some other person, such as his good-humoured charm. The objects and their qualities which can cause pride (to take that emotion only) are many and varied; we may be proud of the beauty of our country, and of the honesty of our children. Bearing the systematizing procedures of natural philosophy in mind, Hume says that it would not be sensible to suppose that human nature is so constituted that different principles are at work here, as though one feature of the mind made beauty a cause of pride, another honesty. These different causes of pride surely must 'partake of some general quality, that naturally operates on the mind'; pride must be explicable by reference to some general principles of human nature.

This general quality is that all the causes of pride, when taken in themselves, are also causes of pleasure. Like any beautiful country, our own will give us pleasure. Given this, the production of pride can now be explained by appeal to the principles of association of impressions, and of ideas. Since 'resembling' impressions are apt to lead to each other, the pleasure we feel in a beautiful country is apt, depending on the circumstances and details of the case, to lead to emotions such as love, generosity, pride, and courage. Where the country is ours it will lead to pride; for the idea of its being ours will lead, by association, to the idea of ourselves, which is the 'object' of pride. As Hume says, 'the one idea [of the house being mine] is easily converted into its correlative [the idea of myself]; and the one impression [of pleasure] into that [pride], which resembles and corresponds to it.' The same mechanism applies to the other indirect passions. Like pride or its converse, humility, love and hatred 'resemble' pleasure and pain, but unlike pride and humility, love and hatred have as their 'object', not ourselves, but some other person.

Having dealt, by appeal to the same observed principles of human nature, with both 'the understanding' and the non-moral passions, Hume turns to the third part of his study of man, to 'morals', 'a subject that interests us above all others'. This amounts to studying those calm impressions of reflection which are the delights and satisfactions we take in people's virtues and their morally good actions. Such feelings of approval of people's virtues must relate in *some* way to a recognition of them *as* virtues. Exactly how they relate will depend on how it comes about in the first place that we distinguish some things as virtues, others as vices. On the one hand, for example, our recognition of something as a virtue might simply be 'an immediate feeling', a feeling 'founded entirely on the particular fabric and constitution of the human species', like our recognition of some quality as sweet. In this case, the delight and satisfaction which we take in virtue will hardly be more than an immediate emotional reaction. On the other hand, our recognition of something as morally good may be a matter of intuitions and demonstrations of reason, a matter of 'relations of ideas'. In this case the delights and satisfactions we take in virtue will be a product of deliberation and judgement.

Hume, therefore, begins by considering 'a controversy started of late ... concerning the general foundation of Morals; whether they be derived from Reason, or from Sentiment'. According to some, the divisions we make between good and bad, virtue and vice, derive from 'a chain of argument'. Samuel Clarke, for example, held that there is a certain objective moral 'fitness or suitableness of certain circumstances to certain persons ... founded in the nature of things, and ... persons'. Goodness and badness, virtue and vice, are a matter of these objective 'fitnesses' and 'suitablenesses' which, like 'the properties which flow from the essences of different figures' to which Clarke compares them, are discoverable by reason. According to others, such as Francis Hutcheson, the divisions and distinctions of morality do not have their source in an independent moral reality, but are a matter of 'immediate feeling'. The *Treatise* puts the matter by asking 'whether it is by means of our *ideas* or *impressions* we distinguish betwixt vice and virtue, and pronounce an action blameable or praise-worthy'. If the former, then morality is a matter of 're-lations of ideas' and, as Samuel Clarke thought, moral goodness will be a demonstrable matter, like the propositions of arithmetic and geometry. If the latter, it will simply be a more or less immediate matter of emotional feelings and reactions; it will be 'more properly felt than judged of'. His study of the 'understanding' led Hume to conclude that many of our beliefs, those of 'matters of fact', were not based on reason, but were akin to natural instinctive feelings. So it is, he thinks, in the case of our moral evaluations and preferences. The fact that he is able to give a unity to the various aspects of man by accounting for them in the same way, by appeal to the same underlying principles of human nature, is, he rightly suggests, a reason in favour of his views.

Hume accepts that people often engage in arguments about the moral merits of some particular case. He does not accept that this entails that moral distinctions are, after all, a matter of reason. Their engaging in such arguments does not mean that it is not some 'immediate feeling and finer internal sense' which, in the end, decides whether something is worthy of moral approval. Reason may 'pave the way for such a sentiment', for it may point out unnoticed features or consequences of an action and help us to compare and contrast it with others, but ultimately our praise and blame is a matter of emotion, feeling, or sentiment. For one thing, 'what is honourable, what is fair, what is becoming, what is noble, what is generous, takes possession of the heart', and reason cannot do this. As he argued in connection with free will, reason can tell us how best to attain a desired end, but it cannot give us those desires which move us to action. But 'morals' do 'excite passions, and produce or prevent actions', and so its divisions and distinctions 'are not conclusions of our reason'. Hume's most fundamental argument for the idea that reason 'is wholly inactive, and can never be the source of so active a principle as conscience, or a sense of morals' is that reason has to do with the discovery of truth and falsehood, whereas our passions, volitions, and actions are neither true nor false.

That moral distinctions are not a matter of reason but of sentiment or feeling will become clearer, Hume thinks, from particular cases. The two virtues he chooses are 'benevolence', which covers such things as mercy, humaneness, and generosity, and 'justice'. Why do we praise and approve of such things? In the case of benevolence, it is at least *partly* because of its *usefulness*, both to ourselves and others. 'Nothing can bestow more merit on any human creature than the sentiment of benevolence in an eminent degree; and ... a *part*, at least, of its merit arises from its tendency to promote the interests of our species, and bestow happiness on human society.' The other element in our praise of benevolence stems from its being pleasing in itself. Hume contrasts the 'softness and tenderness', the 'engaging endearments', the 'fond expressions' of benevolence, with the 'roughness and harshness' of 'perpetual wrangling, and scolding'. The latter 'disturb and displease', the former communicate themselves to us and we 'melt ... into the same fondness and delicacy'.

While 'utility' partly accounts for our praise of benevolence, it wholly accounts for our praise of justice. It is the sole foundation of the merit we find in justice, and this is shown by our imagining circumstances in which considerations of justice would not arise. If, 'without any care or industry on our part, every individual finds himself fully provided with whatever his most voracious appetites can want', there would be no need for rules of justice to apportion things or consider people's rights. If, to take another case, people were so benevolent 'that every man has the utmost tenderness for every man, and feels no more concern for his own interest than for that of his fellows', then 'the use of justice would be suspended ... [and] the divisions and barriers of property and obligation [would never] have been thought of '. We see from this that the sole merit of justice is its 'utility'. 'By rendering justice totally *useless*, you thereby totally destroy its essence, and suspend its obligation upon mankind.'

But why does 'utility' excite our praise and approval? Hume is in no doubt that it does so, not because of education and training, but because of some *natural* propensity of the mind. He denies, however, what this might seem to suggest, that the propensity is based on self-interest. We do not value benevolence in a person because of its benefit *to us*. The moral value we place on justice is not that *we* cannot fail to benefit from it in the long run. Of course, we are favourably disposed to whatever tends to our own advantage, but such feelings are different from our 'general affection for virtue'. We can approve of benevolent and just acts when others benefit, and even when we ourselves stand to lose.

Hume's view, then, is that moral approval is an essentially disinterested and selfless matter. Benevolence is praised, at least partly, because of its usefulness. But usefulness to whom? Not to ourselves, but to whomever, on the particular occasion, it happens to be useful. The fact that we are not indifferent to the welfare and benefits of *other* people strikes Hume as a principle of human nature of great importance, for it is 'one great source of moral distinctions'. The discovery that we can, as a disinterested, unselfish matter, take into consideration the welfare and happiness of other people, is the discovery of 'a principle, which accounts, in great part, for the origin of morality'. To Hume it is an undeniable fact, and one in complete antithesis to Hobbes's egocentric view of human nature, that it is 'impossible for such a creature as man to be totally indifferent to the well- or ill-being of his fellow-creatures'.

In the *Enquiry*, the principle that humans are capable of such disinterested feelings is left as a basic feature of their nature. The *Treatise*, however, derives it, in terms of the notion of 'sympathy', from other, previously discovered, principles such as those of association. 'Sympathy' is also used to explain the other feature in our approval of benevolence, which is its communicating itself to us and being pleasing in itself. Hume's 'sympathy' is not itself a feeling or impression. It is not the same as 'pity', an emotion which is itself explained in terms of sympathy. It is a mental mechanism by which the feelings of other people, 'however different from, or contrary to our own' are communicated to us, so that we have them ourselves. Though Hume might better have called it 'empathy', for sympathy is usually thought of as the having of feelings *suitable to*, rather than *identical with*, those of others, it is, he thinks, more likely than 'any influence of the soil and climate' to account for the character of a nation, that is, for the uniformity in feeling of its people. Noting that the happiness of another person communicates itself to the company he is with, Hume explains that what has happened is that the *idea* we have of his feelings, an idea given to us by 'external signs in the countenance and conversation', is enlivened and converted into an *impression*, into the emotion of happiness itself. What is the mechanism of this? From where is the extra liveliness derived? We have, says Hume, a lively impression or permanent consciousness of ourselves. As a consequence, anything related to us by cause and effect, resemblance, or contiguity, will be conceived with the same vivacity. Thus, to take only the second of these, there is a 'great resemblance among all human creatures', and this serves to 'convey the impression or consciousness of our own person to the idea of the sentiments or passions of others, and makes us conceive them in the strongest and most lively manner'.

Justice is valued purely for its utility; circumstances can be imagined in which it would be completely unnecessary. This makes it into an 'artificial' virtue. In many cases, Hume says, actions are virtuous because of the motives which produce them. In the case of justice, however, this is not so. The motive of generosity or benevolence, for example, might lead us to do something quite contrary to justice, such as giving money to the needy which is already owed to some rich man. Apart from the general rules of justice formulated by society, there might be no virtue in my repaying what I owe. The benefits and utility of justice are 'not the consequence of every individual single act', but they arise 'from the whole scheme or system'. In a very attractive metaphor, Hume compares the utility arising from benevolence to 'a wall, built by many hands, which still rises by each stone that is heaped upon it', whereas that of justice is like 'a vault, where each individual stone would, of itself, fall to the ground'. The rules of justice, though on particular occasions working against what generosity or benevolence would indicate, form a 'whole fabric supported ... by the mutual assistance and combination of its corresponding parts'.

According to Hume, then, 'morality is determined by senti-ment'. The moral distinctions of virtue and vice, goodness and badness, are based, not on reason, but on feeling. 'Virtue ... is whatever mental actions or quality gives to a spectator the pleas-ing sentiment of approbation; and vice the contrary.' This approbation is essentially disinterested; not 'every sentiment of pleasure or pain, which arises from character and actions [is] of that *peculiar* kind, which makes us praise and condemn'. It is only when we consider these 'in general, without reference to our own particular interest, that it causes such a feeling or sentiment, as denominates it morally good or evil'.

In the Introduction to the *Treatise*, Hume explained that 'all the sciences have a relation, greater or less, to human nature'. Even religion, he said, is dependent on moral science, since it lies 'under the cognizance of men, and ... [is] judged of by their powers and faculties'. Having looked at his science of man, we must now look at some of what he says about religion. Apart from a piece on 'Miracles', which, though it was written for the *Treatise*, made its first appearance in the *First Enquiry*, this is contained in the *Dialogues concerning Natural Religion*.

In Chapter 6 we noted the emergence, in the second half of the seventeenth century, of a belief in the possibility of 'natural religion', a religion based on man's ordinary intellectual capa-cities, which did not need, and even rejected, external help from revelation. One of Hume's main concerns is, in effect, to assess this possibility, and it is one for which his study of 'human under-standing' has paved the way. Are our religious beliefs 'natural' and 'instinctive'? Are they produced by principles which are 'per-manent, irresistible, and universal', and so unchangeable by sceptical argument? Or are they produced by principles which are 'neither unavoidable to mankind, nor necessary', and so such as may be 'easily subverted by a due contrast and opposition'? Are religious beliefs akin to specialized philosophical beliefs, such as that in substantial forms, or are they much the same, in the grounds we have for them, as ordinary everyday 'matter of fact' beliefs? Can scepticism about them produce more conviction than it does about 'matter of fact' beliefs? Is Christian theism a body of philosophical 'fiction', or is it as well-grounded as natural science or mathematics?

Although these questions pervade the *Dialogues on Natural Religion*, Hume's answers are hard to get at. The dialogue form of the work raises the question, which of the three characters—Demea, Cleanthes, or Philo—speaks for Hume. Demea, who is described as rigid, inflexible, and orthodox, holds that a belief in a single Deity with an infinity of perfect, but incomprehensible, attributes can be based on a priori proofs of the kind to be found in mathematics and geometry. Unlike Samuel Clarke, on whose views Demea draws, Hume certainly rejects this, and does not think that religious beliefs are based on 'relations of ideas'. It has been thought that Hume's spokesman is Cleanthes, a man of an 'accurate philosophical turn of mind', whose position was that of supposing that Christian beliefs are not only as well-founded as the 'matter of fact' beliefs of the natural sciences, but have the same foundation in experience. But even if, as seems more likely, Hume's views are those of Philo, a man of 'careless scepticism', it is not completely clear what they are. He certainly agrees with Cleanthes that their discussion ought to avoid a radical scepticism and should proceed on the assumption that ordinary 'matter of fact' beliefs are all right; but how far he agrees that religious beliefs are on a par with them is difficult to measure.

Demea's a priori argument for the existence of God is a version of what is usually known as the Cosmological Argument: in order to find a cause for the world we must, on pain of an infinite regress, 'have recourse to a necessarily-existent Being, who carries the reason of his existence in himself; and who cannot be supposed not to exist without an express contradiction'. It is not discussed at length, and is dismissed quite swiftly on the grounds that anything we can conceive of as existing can also be conceived of as not existing; there is no being whose non-existence implies a contradiction, no being whose existence is demonstrable a priori.

Cleanthes' Argument from Design receives more attention. According to this, we can know not only of the existence of God, but also something of His nature and properties, on the basis of observation of the world.

Look round the world: contemplate the whole and every part of it: ... The curious adapting of means of ends, throughout all nature, resembles exactly, though it much exceeds, the productions of human contrivance. ... Since therefore the effects resemble each other, we are led to infer, by all the rules of analogy, that the causes also resemble; and that the Author of Nature is somewhat similar to the mind of man; though possessed of much larger faculties, proportioned to the grandeur of the work.

Philo objects to this. Unlike Demea he has no worry about leaving religion unsupported by abstract a priori arguments, and basing it on 'experience and probability'. His worry is that, even by the ordinary standards and canons of empirical belief, canons which are acceptable to all but the philosophical sceptic, the argument is weak. Besides being somewhat vague, the analogy between the universe and a human artefact compares one thing with parts of itself. Could one learn how people reproduce from seeing how their hair grows? Moreover, although human intelligence is the cause of some things, why build anything on this fact? Why make 'this little agitation of the brain which we call *thought* ... the model of the whole universe'?

But even though Philo purports to be avoiding radical philosophical scepticism of the sort which questions naturally formed beliefs, Cleanthes feels that his objections must really come from 'the most perverse, obstinate metaphysics' and scepticism. For their observation of the world simply does lead people to the thought of an intelligent designer. If one considers the structure and contrivance of the eye, surely, 'from your own feeling ... the idea of a contriver immediately flow[s] in upon you with a force like that of sensation'.

Philo makes no direct reply to this point. He argues, instead, that it does not justify the *details* of Cleanthes' conclusion. We could as easily have the idea that the world was created by an intelligence with a body, or by a number of intelligences, or by a finite intelligence; or perhaps the world is self-sustaining like an animal, with God as its animating soul. If we follow Cleanthes' argument, says Philo, we may be 'able, perhaps, to assert, or conjecture, that the universe . . . arose from something like design; but beyond that position he cannot ascertain one single circumstance, and is left to fix every point of his theology, by the utmost licence of fancy and hypothesis'. Is Philo, on behalf of Hume, reducing Cleanthes' Argument from Design to absurdity and rejecting it out of hand? It would seem not, for at the end of the *Dialogues* he appears to accept that religious belief of a somewhat indeterminate kind is supported by the impression of design that the world really does give.

Hume has been rated very highly as an 'empiricist' by the Logical Positivists in our own century, and he is often given as an exemplar of the type. Several of his views seem to justify this reputation. His claim that the meaningfulness of any word can be established only by relating it to impressions given in experience, and his refusal to go along with Berkeley and Malebranche in asking questions about the causes of those impressions, have already been remarked upon. To these could be added his denial that there is any intelligible connection between causes and effects, and his rejection of reason as a factor in the formation of our factual beliefs and moral evaluations. But the very style and underlying tendency of his philosophy should also be taken into account. From the start, his dispassionate programme of coolly observing human nature at work, and his modest Newtonian aim of finding some few systematizing principles, which themselves are taken at face value and left unexplained, mark him out as someone reluctant to go beyond experience, and wary of approaching the world with preconceived theories.

References

Abbreviations

BD   George Berkeley, *Dialogues*. References are to Dialogues and numbered divisions.

BI   —— 'Introduction' to his *Principles*. References are to paragraphs.

BP   —— *Principles*. References are to paragraphs.

BV   —— *New Theory of Vision*. References are to paragraphs.

Quotations from all the above works by Berkeley are taken from *Berkeley: Philosophical Writings*, ed. M. R. Ayers (London, 1975).

BW   *The Works of Francis Bacon* (Stuttgart, 1961–3): reproduction in facsimile of the *Works*, ed. James Spedding, R. L. Ellis, and D. D. Heath (London, 1857–74), and of *Letters and Occasional Works*, ed. James Spedding (London, 1861). References are to volumes and pages.

GI   *Pierre Gassendi's Institutio Logica, 1658*, trans. and ed. Howard Jones (Assen, 1981). References are to pages.

GS   *The Selected Works of Pierre Gassendi*, trans. and ed. Craig B. Brush (New York and London, 1972). References are to pages.

HE   David Hume, *Enquiries Concerning Human Understanding and Concerning the Principles of Morals*, ed. L. A. Selby-Bigge (3rd edn., Oxford, 1975). References are to the first or second Enquiry, followed by sections and parts.

HN   —— *Dialogues on Natural Religion* in *Hume on Religion*, ed. Richard Wollheim (London, 1963). References are to sections and pages.

HT   —— *Treatise of Human Nature*, ed. L. A. Selby-Bigge (2nd edn., Oxford, 1978). References are to books, sections, and parts.

HW   *The English Works of Thomas Hobbes*, ed. William Molesworth (London, 1839-45; reprinted Aalen, 1962). References are to volumes and pages.

LE   John Locke, *Essay Concerning Human Understanding*: the partially modernized quotations are from P. H. Nidditch's authoritative edition (Oxford, 1975). References are to books, chapters, and sections.

LT —— *Two Treatises of Government*: the partially modernized quotations are from Peter Laslett's critical edition (Cambridge, 1960). References are to sections.

Chapter 1

1. *one of the great*: Bertrand Russell, *The Problems of Philosophy* (London, 1912: reprinted 1959), p. 41.
5. *men have been*: BW iv. 81–2.
   Philosophy and the: BW iv. 14.
6. *that wisdom*: BW iv. 14.
   what is it else: John Webster, *Academiarum Examen* (London, 1653: reprinted in A. G. Debus, *Science and Education in the Seventeenth Century* (London and New York, 1970)), p. 15.

Chapter 2

9. *whatsoever nature*: BW i. 3.
10. *wealth, precedence*: Lord Macaulay, *Critical and Historical Essays* (London, 1866), ii. 316.
    Snow lay: John Aubrey, *Brief Lives*, ed. Anthony Powell (London, 1949), p. 192.
    cold preserves: BW iv. 137.
    the general language: BW xiv. 434.
    a citizen: BW xiv. 436.
    I have taken all: BW viii. 109.
11. *wet weather*: BW v. 157.
    there is no medium: BW iv. 202.
    islanders generally: BW v. 257.
12. *inspired by*: BW iv. 336.
    is like the sun: BW iv. 20.
    Men must soberly: BW vi. 753.
13. *Let a man look*: BW iv. 13–14.
14. *doomed men*: BW iv. 75.
    hence the fiction: BW iv. 55.
15. *rely solely; pure reasoners; out of their own; mere medley; from the flowers; league; much may be*: BW iv. 93.
    to experience: BW iv. 94.
    The information: BW iv. 26.

16. *snatch from*: BW iv. 63–4.
     first fell into: BW i. 4.
     made his natural: BW iv. 59.
     demonstration by: BW iv. 24.
17. *but one course*: BW iv. 8.
     It is necessary: BW iv. 18.
     true and natural: BW iv. 115.
18. *a summary*: BW iv. 22.
     the Phenomena: BW iv. 28.
     for wayside inns; by which the legitimate; both above my strength:
        BW iv. 32.
     True directions: BW iv. 37.
19. *it is like the peace*: BW xiv. 168.
     their optical portions: BW iv. 361.
20. *Essence and Presence; Deviation, or; most akin*: BW iv. 129.
     Degrees or Comparison: BW iv. 137.
21. *Supports and Rectifications*: BW iv. 247.
     as is always: BW iv. 145.
     the way to come; there will remain: BW iv. 146.
     indulgence to: BW iv. 154.
     Prerogative Instance: BW iv. 155.
     shining instances: BW iv. 158.
22. *First Vintage*: BW iv. 149.
     displayed most: BW iv. 150.
     a motion, expansive: BW iv. 154.
     commence a total: BW iv. 8.
     men of experiment: BW iv. 92.
23. *the entire work*: BW iv. 40.
24. *it was the ambitious*: BW iv. 20.
     either for pleasure: BW iv. 21.
25. *the inward glory; end or scope*: BW i. 7.
26. *the interpreting of*: BW iii. 127.
     The End of our: BW iii. 156.
     better liked: Aubrey, op. cit. (note to p. 10), p. 242.

Chapter 3

28. *solitary, poor*: HW iii. 113.
     ripened and: HW ii. xx.
     was rather a dream: HW iii. 668.
     I believe that scarce: HW iii. 669.
     content themselves: HW i. 2.

29. *Most men wander*: HW i. 1–2.
30. *in love with*: Aubrey, op. cit. (note to p. 10), p. 242.
    opened to us: HW i. viii.
31. *such knowledge*: HW i. 3.
33. *Sense and Memory*: HW i. 3.
    History ... most useful: HW i. 10.
36. *indefinite science*: HW i. 68.
37. *universal things; the causes of*: HW i. 69.
    space which is; the privation of; the motion of a point: HW i. 70.
    those that say: HW i. 531.
38. *the motion of a line*: HW i. 70.
    kind of contemplation; the consideration of; what way, and: HW i. 71.
    Of all the phenomena: HW i. 389.
39. *nothing but the*: The Philosophical Works of Descartes, trans. E. S. Haldane and G. R. T. Ross (Cambridge, 1931), ii. 65.
    the reaction: HW i. 391.
    If a cause: HW i. 72.
40. *There is no effect*: HW vii. 88.
    by the appearances: HW i. 388.
41. *motions of the mind*: HW i. 72.
    the original of life; the fountain of sense: HW i. 406.
42. *by a certain impulsion*: HW ii. 8.
43. *by the experience*: HW i. 73.
    unless they be; may be known: HW i. 74.
    grounded on its own: HW ii. xx.
44. *The science of every*: HW vii. 184.
    consider men: HW ii. 109.
    we are the matter: HW iii. x.
45. *in such a condition*: HW iii. 113.
    The dispositions of men: HW ii. xiv–xv.
    Covenants, without: HW iii. 154.
    I authorize and give up: HW iii. 158.
46. *that men know*: HW i. 8.
    conscientious obedience: HW vii. 336.
    to think the worse: HW vii. 6.
47. *most commodious*: HW ii. xxii.
    an incorporeal substance: HW iii. 393.
    extraordinarily advanced: HW i. ix.
    they loved each other: Aubrey, op. cit. (note to p. 10), p. 258.

Chapter 4

48. *the sweetest-natured*: Aubrey, op. cit. (note to p. 10), p. 258.
49. *the vanity as well as*: GS 19.
50. *in this matter*: GS 28.
52. *Definition . . . reveals*: Aristotle, *Posterior Analytics*, 91a 1 (quoted from vol. 1 of W. D. Ross (ed.), *The Works of Aristotle* (London, 1908–52)).
53. *a thing's characteristic*: Thomas Aquinas, *Summa Theologiae*, 3a.75, 6 (quoted from vol. 58 of the Blackfriars' edition (London, 1964–75)).
54. *Just what routes*: GS 33.
    does not reveal: GS 34.
    What qualities: GS 98.
    You will surely: GS 78.
55. *You may say*: GS 78–9.
    Indeed, if Aristotle: GS 83.
56. *painstaking experience*: GS 36.
    Experience is the balance: GS 40.
    learning and human: GS 24.
    really persuade: GS 20.
    our experience shows; that fire is hot: GS 87.
    they have senses: GS 305.
57. *inner natures*: GS 104.
    it becomes apparent: GS 101–2.
    When a mathematician: GS 106.
    persist in regarding: GS 86.
58. *allow that a certain*: GS 86.
    not belong to the party: GS 101.
    it may well be; *a knowledge of experience*; *that there are some*; *can proceed no farther*: GS 104.
    the labours of: GS 105.
60. *the inner nature*; *they are not speaking*: GS 294.
61. *the truth itself*; *yearn to fly*: GS 327.
    The truth in question: GS 329.
    become evident; *cannot become perceptible*: GS 290.
    sweat is of such: GS 332.
62. *he will be considered*: GS 341–2.
    the underlying component: GS 190–1.
    underground spring: GS 200.
64. *Clear thinking*: GS 351.
    general precepts: GS 349.
    Every idea; *deprived of every sense*: GI 84–5.

65.   *is in the senses*: GS 86.
      The senses ... ultimately: GI 160.
      the innate force: GS 30.

Chapter 5

68.   *kept in nonage*: Abraham Cowley, prefatory ode in Thomas Sprat,
      *History of the Royal Society for the improving of Natural
      Knowledge* (London, 1667: copied in facsimile, London, 1959,
      ed. J. I. Cope and H. W. Jones).
70.   *a prophetic scheme*: Joseph Glanvill, *Scepcis Scientifica* (London,
      1665: copied in facsimile as vol. 3 (1985) of *Collected Works of
      Joseph Glanvill* (Hildesheim & New York)), introduction.
      had the true imagination; *are every where scattered*: Sprat, op. cit.
      (note to p. 68), p. 35.
      all the main heads: Glanvill, *Plus Ultra* (London, 1668: copied in
      facsimile as vol. 4 (1979) of the collection cited above), p. 75.
      one of the first: Robert Boyle, *The Works*, ed. T. Birch (London,
      1772: copied in facsimile, Hildesheim, 1966), v. 514.
      the science of nature: Robert Hooke, *Micrographia* (London, 1665:
      reprinted, New York, 1961), p. 5.
      lay a new foundation: Henry Power, *Experimental Philosophy ...
      in illustration of the new atomical hypothesis* (London, 1664),
      p. 192.
      by enlarging the history: Glanvill, *Plus Ultra*, p. 9.
      fundamentally necessary: ibid., p. 51.
      faithful records: Sprat, op. cit. (note to p. 68), p. 61.
71.   *Men that are much*: Méric Casaubon, *Letter to Peter du Moulin ...
      concerning natural experimental philosophy* (Cambridge, 1669),
      p. 30.
72.   *nothing to do*; *May not a man*; *profited more*; *to gratify*: ibid., p. 34.
      idle boys who; *cut off and deny*: Richard Baxter, *Reasons of the
      Christian Religion* (London, 1667), p. 498.
73.   *the weightiest*: Sprat, op. cit. (note to p. 68), p. 345.
      The knowledge of: Boyle, op. cit. (note to p. 70), ii. 30.

Chapter 6

75.   *examine our own*: LE, 'Epistle to the Reader'.
      enquire into: LE 1. 1. 2.
      principles of morality: James Tyrrell, manuscript note in his copy of
      LE (British Museum, C. 122, f. 14).
      despair of: LE 1. 1. 6.
      raise questions; *horizon ... between*; *with less scruple*: LE 1. 1. 7.

76. *Men have reason*: LE 1. 1. 5.
    yearn to fly: GS 327.
    our business: LE 1. 1. 6.
    How comes; *I answer*: LE 2. 1. 2.
77. *general propositions*: Henry Lee, *Anti-Scepticism: or notes upon each chapter of Mr. Locke's Essay* (1702), p. 43.
78. *owe their clearness*: James Lowde, *Discourse concerning the Nature of Man* (1694), p. 57.
79. *white paper*: LE 2. 1. 2.
    Our senses: LE 2. 1. 3.
    perception of the: LE 2. 1. 4.
    All those sublime: LE 2. 1. 24.
80. *whatsoever is the*: LE 1. 1. 8.
81. *observed to exist*; *Abstraction*: LE 2. 12. 1.
    Space, Time: LE 2. 12. 8.
    the perception of; *perceive that*: LE 4. 1. 2.
    in some of our: LE 4. 3. 29.
    immediately . . . without: LE 4. 2. 1.
82. *find out some*: LE 4. 2. 2.
    though we may fancy: LE 4. 1. 2.
    a want of: LE 4. 3. 28.
    conceive . . . [the: LE 4. 3. 29.
83. *the contemplation of*: LE 4. 6. 13.
84. *experimental knowledge*: LE 4. 3. 29.
    natural philosophy: LE 4. 12. 10.
    the way of experiments: Thomas Sergeant, *The Method to Science* (London, 1696), preface.
85. *led . . . to something*: LE 2. 25. 1.
    things subsisting: LE 2. 12. 6.
89. *distinct particular*; *the supposed*: LE 2. 12. 6.
    substratum: LE 2. 23. 1.
    pure substance: LE 2. 23. 2.
    an extended solid: LE 2. 23. 22.
90. *the nature of matter*: René Descartes, *Principles of Philosophy*, 2. 4. (quoted from Haldane and Ross, op. cit. (note to p. 39), i. 255–6).
    in our mode: ibid., i. 260.
    solid parts: LE 2. 23. 23.
91. *contain not in*: LE 2. 12. 4.
    scattered and: LE 2. 22. 1.
    creatures of the: LE 3. 5. 12.
    as they have frequent: LE 2. 22. 5.
92. *figure including*: LE 3. 3. 18.

93. *then the properties*: LE 2. 31. 6
   certain and universal: LE 4. 3. 29.
   Substances afford: LE 4. 12. 9.
94. *its great and proper*: Locke, *Works* (London, 1883: reprinted Aalen, 1963), vii. 140.
95. *The Gospel ... contains*: *The Correspondence of John Locke*, ed. E. S. de Beer (Oxford, 1976–   ), v. 595.
   cannot know: Locke, op. cit. (note to p. 94), vii. 146.
   be to subvert: LE 4. 18. 5.
96. *by the natural use; that the dead*: LE 4. 18. 7.
   but whether it be: LE 4. 18. 10.
   given all mankind: LE 3.9. 23.
   the late extravagant: Sprat, op. cit. (note to p. 68), p. 375.
   the fierceness of: ibid., p. 374.
97. *ungrounded fancies*: LE 4. 19. 3.
   the conceits: LE 4. 19. 7.
   how great soever: LE 4. 19. 10.
98. *a colt grown up*: LE 2. 27. 3.
   partake of the same: LE 2. 27. 4.
   the ordinary way: LE 2. 27. 15.
   nothing but a: LE 2. 27. 6.
   a thinking, intelligent: LE 2. 27. 9.
   will be the same: LE 2. 27. 10.
   one principal property: Descartes, op. cit. (note to p. 39), i. 240.
   a substance the whole: ibid., i. 101.
99. *power of exciting*: LE 2. 23. 22.
   always thinks: LE 2. 1. 9.
   every drowsy nod: LE 2. 1. 12.
   wherein thinking: LE 4. 3. 6.
   what makes the same; the unity of: LE 2. 27. 10.
100. *It being the same*: LE 2. 27. 10.
   more probable opinion: LE 2. 27. 25.
   since we know not: LE 4. 3. 6.
101. *given to some; [all] the great ends*: LE 4. 3. 6.
   Person ... is a: LE 2. 27. 26.
102. *not himself*: LE 2. 27. 20.
   what is real; no one shall be; conscience [is]: LE 2. 27. 22.
   concerned and accountable: LE 2. 27. 26.
   one intellectual: LE 2. 27. 13.
103. *harm another*: LT 6.
104. *Whatsoever then*: LT 27.
   enter into society; by setting up: LT 89.

105. *the will and*: LT 96.
    the consent of any: LT 99.
    at liberty to go: LT 121.
    the community perpetually: LT 149.
106. *upon every little*: LT 225.
    The People shall: LT 240.
    So wonderfully pleased: de Beer, op. cit. (note to p. 95), iv. 602.

Chapter 7

107. *ev'ry virtue*: Alexander Pope, quoted by A. A. Luce, *The Life of George Berkeley, Bishop of Cloyne* (London, 1949), p. 182.
    humility, tenderness: Anne Berkeley, quoted ibid.
109. *Matter once allow'd*: Berkeley, 'Philosophical Commentaries', entry 625, in vol. i of *The Works of George Berkeley* (London, 1948), ed. A. A. Luce and T. E. Jessop.
    so near and; *furniture of the*; *do not exist in*: BP 6.
110. *supposing a difference*; *then are we*; *so that, for aught*: BP 87.
    immediate object; *but something that*; *It often happens*: Nicolas Malebranche, *The Search after Truth* (1674), trans. Thomas M. Lennon and Paul J. Olscamp (Columbus, Ohio, 1980), p. 217.
111. *a very precarious*; *without any reason*; *should imprint*: BP 19.
    The actual receiving: LE 4. 11. 2.
112. *are perceptions of*; *Why could not*; *their own real*: Pierre Bayle, *Historical and Critical Dictionary* (1697), selections trans. Richard H. Popkin (Indianapolis and New York, 1965), p. 365.
113. *Those immediate objects*; *ideas into things*: BD iii. 244.
    to trust your senses: BD iii. 246.
    though otherwise: HE 1. 12. 1.
    The Irishman who: Gottfried Leibniz, 'Letter to Des Bosses', in L. E. Loemker (ed.), *Leibniz: Philosophical Papers and Letters* (2nd edn., Dordrecht–Holland, 1969), p. 609.
    for we may perhaps: as reported in *Boswell's Life of Johnson*, ed. G. B. Hill (Oxford, 1887), iv. 27.
    We are not for: BP 40.
114. *detracts from*; *is very far from*: BP 36.
    the same principles: BD iii. 263.
    unite[d]and place[d]; *the things immediately*: BD iii. 262.
    it will be objected: BP 42.
115. *being a line*: BV 2.
    judge of distance: BV 24.
    would, at first: BV 41.
    the immediate objects: BV 44.

116. *affected with such*: BV 45.
    A man no more: BV 47.
    we see shame; *let in by*; *without which*: BV 65.
    visible extension: BV 139.
    learnt at our first: BV 144.
117. *The proper objects*: BV 147.
    seem as strange: BV 148.
    esse is percipi; *The table I write*; *should have any*: BP 3.
118. *manifest contradiction*: BP 4.
    evident: BP 1.
119. *all that is real*; *a rerum natura*: BP 34.
    it is not in my power: BP 29.
    more strong, lively; *steadiness, order*: BP 30.
    when we perceive: BP 32.
120. *gives us a sort*: BP 31.
    bodies are annihilated: BP 48.
121. *When I deny*: BD iii. 230.
122. *a nicer strain*: BP 5.
    Surely there is; *The mind, taking*: BP 23.
    figure, motion, and the rest: BP 10.
123. *false principle*: BI 4.
    into uncouth paradoxes: BI 1.
    Besides the external; *the plainest things*: BP 97.
    not a little: BP 100.
124. *nothing in the world*: HW iii. 21.
    never the name; *man, stone, etc.*: HW i. 20.
125. *One universal name*: HW iii. 21.
    obscure and spurious; *great universals*; *that mad opinion*: GS 42–3.
    the universal concept: GS 46.
    come we by; *made the signs*; *separating from them*: LE 3. 3. 6.
    they do not signify: LE 3. 3. 12.
    in the leaving out: LE 3. 3. 9.
126. *general words*; *to which idea*: LE 3. 3. 12.
    general and universal: LE 3. 3. 11.
    those great masters: BI 17.
    Whether others have; *abstract one from*; *frame a general*: BI 10.
    neither line, surface: BI 8.
    wherein, it is true: BI 9.
    made to represent; *how we can know*: BI 16.
127. *The idea I have*; *the diagram I have*: BI 16.
    great source: BP 97.

disputes and speculations: BP 134.

stand for general: BP 100.

are entirely banished: BP 85.

the two great; *exaggerate, and*; *We are miserably*: BP 101.

128. *the result of any*: BP 107.

there is something alike: BP 104.

those qualities: BP 110.

the two great: BP 101.

the errors arising; *that the principles*: BP 118.

129. *abstract ideas*; *subservient to*; *high flights*; *numbers in abstract*: BP 119.

abstractcd from; *particular things*: BP 120.

objects of sense: BP 125.

thought to have; *geometrical paradoxes*; *the principal occasion*: BP 123.

130. *ignorant of*; *manifestly impossible*: BP 135.

spiritual substance: BD iii. 232.

by their operations: BP 145.

a distinct principle; *that whereas some*: BP 148.

main drift: BP 156.

human agents: BP 146.

131. *constant regularity*: BP 146.

Epicureans, Hobbists: BP 93.

How great a friend: BP 92.

one of the greatest: HT 1. 1. 7.

hid . . . behind: Berkeley, *Siris: A Chain of Philosophical Reflexions and Inquiries* (London, 1744), sect. 64.

132. *we do at all times*: BP 148.

Chapter 8

133. *fell dead-born*: Hume, 'My Own Life', *Letters of David Hume*, ed. J. Y. T. Greig (Oxford, 1932), i. 2.

134. *monkish virtues*: HE 2. 9. 2.

There is no question; *march up*; *to explain the principles*: HT Intro.

135. *laid on*; *the application of*; *glean up our*: HT Intro.

experiments to confirm: HT 2. 2. 2.

the greatest and rarest; *cautious in admitting*: Hume, *History of England*, ch. 71.

is a kind of attraction: HT 1. 1. 4.

136. *totally shut up*: HE 1. 4. 1.

intemperate desire; *original qualities*: HT 1. 1. 4.

137. *Impressions . . . ideas*: HT 1. 1. 1.
     Everyone will readily: HE 1. 2.
138. *all the perceptions; is the first principle*: HT 1 . 1. 1.
     Those who would; that a philosophical term: HE 1. 2.
139. *the mind takes*: LE 2. 1. 4.
     appearance in the soul: HT 1. 1. 1.
     the application of: HT 2. 1. 1.
     unknown causes: HT 1. 1. 2.
     perfectly inexplicable; material to our: HT 1. 3. 5.
140. *a gentle force; universal . . . uniting; our imagination; contiguity in
     time; cause and effect; which produces*: HT 1. 1. 4.
     examination of our; principally deserve: HT 1. 1. 2.
141. *passions, desires*: HT 1. 1. 2.
     all the objects; discoverable by; with the same facility; is the nature:
     HE 1. 4. 1.
142. *present testimony; all reasonings; the nature of; enquire how we; are
     discoverable*: HE 1 . 4. 1 .
143. *be extended to; such an object; other objects, which; the supposition;
     causes which appear; no contradiction*: HE 1. 4. 2.
144. *be evidently going; engaged by arguments; the most ignorant; custom
     and habit; such an object*: HE 1. 4. 2.
     produces a propensity: HE 1. 5. 1.
145. *Having found in; is the necessary result*: HE 1. 5. 1.
146. *a species of*: HT 1. 4. 1.
147. *amazement and confusion*: HE 1. 12. 2.
     The intense view; cold, and strained: HT 1. 4. 7.
148. *permanent, irresistible*: HT 1. 1. 4.
     the foundation of all: HT 1. 4. 4.
     linked by a chain: HT 1. 3. 2.
     appears to the outward; any power or; the motion of: HE 1. 7. 1.
149. *The power or energy*: HE 1. 7. 1.
     seem entirely; but we never can; connection . . . which: HE 1. 7. 2.
150. *a reconciling project; A man who at noon; The conjunction between*:
     HE 1. 8. 1.
     transfer the determination: HT 1. 3. 14.
     proceed not from: HT 2. 3. 2.
     the combat of passion: HT 2. 3. 3.
151. *Reason is . . . only; disputing the preference; it is not contrary*: HT 2.
     3. 3.
     a violent and sensible: HT 2. 3. 8.
     launch out into: HT 1. 4. 6.
     a natural impulse: HT 2. 3. 9.

152. *The mind by an*: HT 2. 3. 9.
    whatever other objects: HT 2. 1. 2.
    partake of some: HT 2. 1. 3.
153. *the one idea*: HT 2. 1. 5.
    a subject that: HT 3. 1. 1.
    an immediate feeling; *a controversy started*: HE 2. 1 .
154. *fitness or suitableness*: Samuel Clarke, *A Discourse concerning the Unchangeing Obligations of Natural Religion* (London, 1706: reproduced in facsimile, Stuttgart-Bad Cannstatt, 1964), p. 47.
    whether it is by: HT 3. 1. 1.
    more properly felt: HT 3. 1. 2.
    immediate feeling; *pave the way*: HE 2. 1.
155. *what is honourable*: HE 2. 1.
    excite passions; *is wholly inactive*: HT 3. 1. 1.
    Nothing can bestow: HE. 2. 2. 2.
    softness and tenderness; *disturb and displease*: HE 2. 7.
    without any care: HE 2. 3. 1 .
156. *that every man*; *By rendering justice*: HE 2. 3. 1.
    general affection; *one great source*: HE 2. 5. 1 .
    a principle, which; *impossible for such*: HE 2. 5. 2.
157. *however different*; *any influence of*; *external signs*; *great resemblance*: HT 2. 1. 11.
    not the consequence: HE 2. Appendix 3.
158. *a wall, built*; *whole fabric*: HE 2. Appendix 3.
    morality is determined; *Virtue ... is*: HE 2. Appendix 1.
    every sentiment; *in general, without*: HT 3. 1. 2.
    permanent, irresistible: HT 1. 4. 4.
159. *neither unavoidable*: HT 1. 4. 4.
    accurate philosophical; *careless scepticism*: HN Intro.
    have recourse to: HN 9. 162.
160. *Look round the world*: HN 2. 115–16.
    experience and probability: HN 2. 116.
    this little agitation: HN 2. 121.
    the most perverse; *from your own*: HN 3. 128.
161. *able, perhaps, to*: HN 5. 142.

Further Reading

For a key to the abbreviations, together with a full list of the major source-books used in this volume, see the beginning of the References section (p. 162).

Chapter 2: Francis Bacon

There are selections from Bacon's work in Hugh C. Dick, *Selected Writings of Francis Bacon* (New York, 1955), and Arthur Johnson, *Francis Bacon* (London, 1965). *The Advancement of Learning* and *New Atlantis* are available in an Oxford 'World's Classics' volume (London, 1906). Catherine Bowen, *Francis Bacon: The Temper of a Man* (Boston, 1963), is a recent biography. The Oxford 'Past Masters' series contains a very useful volume on Bacon by Anthony Quinton (1980).

Chapter 3: Thomas Hobbes

R. S. Peters, *Hobbes* (Harmondsworth, 1956), provides a systematic account of Hobbes's ideas, while A. P. Martinich, *A Hobbes Dictionary* (Oxford, 1995) is a very useful aid to reading and study. David Boonin-Val, *Thomas Hobbes and the Science of Moral Virtue* (Cambridge, 1994) relates his moral views to his science, and Miriam M. Reik, *The Golden Lands of Thomas Hobbes* (Detroit, 1977) is an intellectual biography.

Chapter 4: Pierre Gassendi

The only selection in English of Gassendi's work is that by Brush (GS). As it contains only some parts of the *Syntagma*, it can, to an extent, be supplemented by Jones (GI), which has more of its Logic. Brush's and Jones's introductions provide very useful discussions, to which Jones's *Pierre Gassendi 1592–1655: An Intellectual Biography* (Nieuwkoop, 1983) is a good background. There is not a great amount on Gassendi in English, but Lynn Sunida Joy's *Gassendi the Atomist* (Cambridge, 1989), and Margaret J. Osler's *Divine Will and the Mechanical Philosophy* (Cambridge, 1994), though not introductory, are excellent.

Chapter 5: The Royal Society of London for the Improving of Natural Knowledge

Sprat's *History* is very readable, and is accessible in a photo-reprint.

Henry Lyons, *The Royal Society 1660-1940* (New York, 1968), and Margery Purver, *The Royal Society: Concept and Creation* (London, 1967), are more recent histories of the Society. Richard F. Jones, *Ancients and Moderns: A Study of the Rise of the Scientific Movement in Seventeenth-Century England* (St Louis, 1961), and R. S. Westfall, *Science and Religion in Seventeenth-Century England* (New Haven, 1958), are absorbing accounts of the period.

Chapter 6: John Locke

Locke's works are readily available in various editions. A full-length biography is provided by M. Cranston, *John Locke: A Biography* (London and New York, 1957). John Dunn, *Locke* (1984, Oxford 'Past Masters' series) discusses in equal length Locke's epistemology and metaphysics, and his political philosophy. The beginning student will be aided by the very sympathetic analysis of some of Locke's central ideas in E. J. Lowe, *Locke on Human Understanding* (London, 1995), and by John W. Yolton, *A Locke Dictionary* (Oxford, 1993). R. S. Woolhouse, *Locke* (Brighton, 1983) treats in more detail some of the themes in this chapter.

Chapter 7: George Berkeley

Beside Ayers's edition, Berkeley's *Principles* and *Dialogues* are available in a Penguin paperback, edited by R. S. Woolhouse (Harmondsworth, 1987). David Berman, *George Berkeley: Idealism and the Man* (Oxford, 1994) is a recent intellectual biography. The Oxford 'Past Masters' series contains an excellent volume on Berkeley by J. O. Urmson, published in the composite volume *British Empiricists* (Oxford, 1992); Jonathan Dancy, *Berkeley: An Introduction* (Oxford, 1987), too, is very helpful to the beginning student. I. C. Tipton's valuable *Berkeley: The Philosophy of Immaterialism* (London, 1974) is a well-documented and exhaustive account of its topic.

Chapter 8: David Hume

The editions of Hume by Selby-Bigge (HE, HT) and Wollheim (HN) are easily obtainable. E. C. Mosner, *The Life of David Hume* (Edinburgh and Oxford, 1954 and 1970), is a standard biography. Terence Penelhum, *Hume* (London, 1975), A. J. Ayer, *Hume* (1980, Oxford 'Past Masters' series), and J. J. Jenkins, *Understanding Hume* (Edinburgh, 1992) are good introductions to Hume's philosophy.

Index